People of Print

PEOPLE OF PRINT

Innovative, Independent Design and Illustration

Marcroy Smith
Andy Cooke

With 452 illustrations

PRINT ISN'T DEAD

Introduction
Marcroy Smith

As the director of People of Print, I feel extremely privileged to have met and worked alongside the most extraordinary collection of artists and print practitioners across the globe. Ever since my first day in the print studio at Brighton University I have been utterly enthralled by the traditional methods of print; I simply get lost within the process and truly love the finished product, which has the most pleasing visual aesthetic merged with an idea of individuality and soul. I could always be found printing band posters in the screen-print studio or pressing and binding my own zines in the letterpress room. These functional rooms are where creative minds make ideas tangible.

After freelancing as a designer and illustrator, interning at a print studio in Brooklyn and working for a design agency in Manhattan, I figured out what my passion was. It was meeting new people, discovering new things, learning while always creating and collaborating along the way. This is what solidified the essence of the online resource People of Print to me and is what inspired the creation of a daily-updated blog, a design-based Department Store and a Directory, in order to share this knowledge and collection of talent with the rest of the world.

Every designer has a different way of designing, every printer has a different way of printing and everybody has different things they want to design and/or print. This book is a collection of those people.

Hackney
Downs
Studios
Russet
Green Shops
every Sunday
& Studios

Part 1: **Essays
Interviews
Visits**

The Story of PoP
Marcroy Smith

People of Print began in 2008, when it was originally developed by Marcroy Smith as an online creative library. Since then, the company has been pushed in many interesting and exciting directions, both online and offline.

Recognizing print as a core process within the creative industries, People of Print is a world-leading online community and directory of creatives who use the medium of print and companies that offer the service of print in all forms. Hence it has become an extremely prestigious platform on which to be mentioned and get noticed.

People of Print acts as a source of inspiration for creatives through its daily curated selection of Web content and its quarterly publication titled *Print Isn't Dead*, uncovering and sharing the work, services, events and more from the world's leading contemporary creatives and the hottest budding talent.

This has proven to be a valuable resource for individual professionals, universities and established design studios.

It also has a curated online shop called Department Store, selling design-based goods from various vendors, whereby it offers affordable selling fees and takes a small commission on sales. PoP's online presence has paved the way for many amazing things to happen in the tangible world.

Through collaborating with numerous studios, agencies, shops and companies, People of Print has been able to create and facilitate extremely impressive solutions for corporate clients, charities and educational and cultural institutions, while continually developing its global community in the world of print.

Projects to date

2011: *Victoria Dalston, London* Live screen printing, linocut, spoken word and music event.

2012: *Pick Me Up, Somerset House, London* Exhibition, print sales, various print workshops.

2012: *KK Outlet, London* Educational printing workshops, exhibition, teaching D&AD students.

2012: *Levi's Flagship Store, Regent Street, London* Working alongside WPS and Exposure to facilitate a five-week live T-shirt printing workshop in-store during the Olympics, printing the artwork of Anthony Burrill.

2012: *Node, Design Museum, London* Working alongside Chris Haughton to project-manage the fair trade 18x18 rug project, exhibition of the carpets in the 1.5 Gallery and their sale via the Design Museum Shop.

2013: *Kipepeo, Kibera, Kenya* Facilitating the production of hand screen-printed greetings cards in the slums of Kibera by setting up a lo-fi functional screen-print studio.

2013: *Fedrigoni, Imaginative Papers Studio, London* Facilitating the first of a series of live workshops demonstrating

[1] Druckfest 2011, CM Series

[2] Ink tests

[3] Lasercut logo

[4] Screen exposure for Fedrigoni workshop

and celebrating the quality of Fedrigoni paper and how it works with ink. Live printing A2 Anthony Burrill posters with neon inks.

2013: *V&A Museum for MasterCard, London* Live T-shirt printing in the main area of the V&A, workshops and exclusive commissioned designs from our trusted network of illustrators.

2013: *Design Museum, London* Working alongside Double Decker to design and print tote bags showing iconic items in the Design Museum; live printing at the opening event.

2014: *London College of Communication* A three-week brief with the students to create an exhibition of A1 printed posters and a process book based around the relationship between analogue and digital.

2014: *Ministry of Sound for vInspired, London* Live garment printing on to recycled clothes, saving clothes from going into landfill.

2014: *Puro Hotels, Poland* Working alongside Double Decker to print original screen-printed posters on to vintage film posters for display in the luxury hotel rooms in Poland.

[5] T-Shirt printing press

[6] Printing workshop for Anthony Burrill

[7] Printing workshop at Levi's, Regent Street

[8] Heretic: guest printing at KK Outlet

Print Is Dead! Long Live Print!
Danielle Pender

From collecting club flyers before I was legally allowed
to enter a club to creating my own magazine, I've always
appreciated a good piece of print. However, rather than
seeing print as something romantic and anachronistic, I
think it's thriving in all aspects of creative and everyday life.
Whether it's the rise in independent publishing, young artists
developing their style with screen prints or established artists
lovingly creating printed matter – print is going through
an interesting period as people find new ways to use it and
experiment with it. With the ever-expanding digital age, will
this continue? Is this just a last hurrah before we all throw
down tools and switch to a totally backlit world? No, I don't
think so. It's not so much a digital vs print argument any
more; it's about appreciating the differences between the
two and celebrating them.

I am the curator at KK Outlet in London, a gallery that
showcases a lot of printed graphic, illustrative and
photographic work. Print is integral to what we do and the
work we exhibit.

Looking at the work of photographers blown up and printed
by fine art printers you have a different experience of the
images. Details, atmosphere and colours call out in ways that
they can't on screen. With screen-printed work, I love the
way that colours layer up; each print is different depending
on the whim of the press and the printer. Supposed mistakes
can make a print more beautiful; there is an element of risk

and reward, whether things turn out as you'd expected or if there's some perceived imperfection. It isn't just about preserving a bygone craft that bears no relevance to the modern age. Print is just as relevant today as it's always been. It tells us something about where we've been, what we value and how we want to be remembered in the future.

What will remain of your blog in thirty years? Digital archiving is yet to be fully addressed, and more young people are choosing to create small-run publications and zines to communicate ideas. You just need to look at the thriving independent publishing scene to see that print is very much not dead. The people behind each successful indie title are passionate, not only about their content but also about the printing processes they use and the stock they select. This passion is matched by the reader who buys their print products as things to keep and cherish. These magazines aren't meant as just vessels to disseminate news and ideas; these are beautiful publications, in some cases on a par with limited-edition art books.

Print offers a different experience altogether. It's sensory, the smell and the feel each add something different to the content. Something committed to print holds more weight in the eye of the reader than something online.

As well as working at KK Outlet I'm also the founder and editor of *Riposte*, a smart magazine for women. I've found that the curation of content in a print product is also more considered. With *Riposte* there is a definite editorial consideration in some circumstances that the subject would work online but that it's not strong enough for the print magazine. Producing a magazine, book or even newspaper today is sometimes a costly venture: whatever is committed to the page needs to be worth it, and I think this is reflected in the way the reader reacts to it. I think the challenge remains creating a business model that fits with the modern age. The production and distribution of print still feels quite old hat, but with crowd sourcing, selling online and peer-to-peer distribution methods becoming more successful it'll be interesting to see how things develop as people experiment with new models.

Our days are now filled with so much digital noise and information, they're often spent something like this. . . Check your phone the minute you wake up, again on the toilet and again on the train into work, sit in front of a computer all day, check your social media platforms on your lunch break and again on the way home, watch online streaming in the evening and scroll through Twitter in bed minutes before you go to sleep. This constant stream of information has become omnipresent. It's great for keeping up to date on news, events, sneezing cats and what Rihanna's groin has been up to, but I'm not sure we really take it all on board. I don't think this chatter allows us the time and space to really evaluate what we're reading or looking at and what we really think about it all. Just as the rolling twenty-four-hour news actually makes us shut down as it becomes boring and we think we understand what we're hearing, so this constant scrolling of stimulus doesn't make us think deeper or allow us the time to read more about a certain issue, as we're always looking for the next story or hilarious clip to share.

Rather than our digital lives relegating print to obsolescence, they have cemented it as something more valuable, whether magazines, books or art. With the proliferation of art and design blogs you can see incredible work by incredible artists and designers all day long on-screen, but that cannot substitute the experience of seeing work in its physical form.

The process of screen printing is such a skill and the end result never fails to impress. I think screen printing is essential for the development of style for artists, especially younger artists. In a life spent in front of a computer screen there's a huge reward in getting your hands dirty and actually producing something tangible. You can't underestimate the feeling of seeing your work as a physical product. This low-cost but massively rewarding process gives artists the opportunity to re-evaluate their work off-screen. It also allows people to own art affordably. My walls at home are covered in the prints of people I've worked with over the years at KK Outlet and those whose work I admire from elsewhere.

In the future, what are we going to pass down to the next generations? Maybe in sixty years, with the development of artificial intelligence, we'll just be able to transfer thoughts and experiences through some sort of mind osmosis, but I think that will be a sad day. Humans are tactile beings, they understand through touch. They also understand, by looking at history, to learn where they've come from, who they are and how to be in the future. I think printed matter, whether magazines, books, photographs or artwork, will prevail because it's part of our make-up, and I think that is something to be celebrated.

Get Your Fix
Andrew Losowsky

I remember the day that print was invented. Graygle had announced it as a stealth product, quietly placing 2D printers into their retail stores. People. Freaked. Out. The first time I played with one, I didn't know what to print. I tried my moniker, giving out a simple throw-up in Times New Roman, sent through the wires to be sprayed on the pulp. My name came out perfect and warm, like bread. It was beautiful.

In their launch video, Graygle listed things they thought people would 2D fix, but they were way off. People went for freeze frames of family videos, kitsch emails of marriage proposals, real-world backups of maps and addresses in case your Graygle chip went down. But as soon as I picked up that moniker, gleaming and fixed for ever on that dried-out, flattened pulp, I knew where I was going. I was going to the streets.

Like thousands of people in that first week, I bought a 2D. They were so cheap because of the ads they fixed each morning, plus they were being touted as the next big thing for backup. I didn't care about backup, I wanted distribution. I started simple, a message to everyone. 'FIX YOUR WORDS' was my first one, a simple pun on 'fixing' things on paper, getting your words out there. I made some glue out of flour and sugar and water from a recipe I found on Graygle Search, which seems kind of ironic now. I fixed a hundred copies, and pasted them around the city. Someone asked me if it was an advertising campaign for the 2D. I told them yes.

It kind of was. Maybe Graygle should have been paying me.

Next I went for something more aggressive, and that's when my own 2D called the police. I should have guessed that every printer would be monitoring its content, I mean why wouldn't it be? As soon as I'd fixed my first poster calling Mayor Ashton 'Major Asscon' . . . well, there was trouble. The funny thing is that the police were notified not because of the message, but because I was using a copyrighted image of her face. I doubled my crime cos underneath the picture I fixed a paragraph about lying and corruption I'd copied out from an ebook – yep, that was copyrighted too. So the police tracked me via my chip, and that was that. But not before I'd put ten of them up around the centre of town, and while I was talking to the cops, the chatter on the net was already going crazy. By the time they'd taken me away, people had started. 2Ds were being used to make public messages, ideas were being fixed and handed out, and sharing in the real world was proving a lot harder to monitor than the virtual one.

I think it was about a week into my jail sentence when people figured out how to disable their 2Ds from communicating with Graygle. The company had it declared an illegal use of their equipment, but it was too late, they were off the grid, no monitoring, no ads. One report said that more than 8,000 2D printers basically just disappeared overnight. By the end of the month, tens of thousands had vanished.

It wasn't long after that when the first open-source 2Ds, with no grid connection at all, went on sale in Myanmar and Thailand, and then the world went crazy.

I was in jail for two months – the two copyright infringements were my second and third strikes, so I didn't even get to speak to a human judge, the system just put me away like it was designed to do. But I knew about the 2D movement, I knew because people outside started to send me printed posters, and stories, and ideas. Someone on the grid said I had started it all, and the grid had not forgotten me. It felt nice.

My release conditions banned me from using a 2D for ten years, but two months later none of that mattered because the earthquake hit, and everything went crazy. With the grid down indefinitely, people needed 2Ds to share information and create communities. The government tried to pass a law saying that all 2Ds had to be restricted for authorized public use, but the corporations quickly put a stop to that precedent being set for their gear, so it ended up how it is today: people can print anything they choose, even copyrighted stuff, as long as they don't try to sell it. And so a million flowers bloomed.

Anyway kiddo, that's my memory of it. Stained pulp became free space, and the grid was left to the companies and the celebrities and the politicians. Just remember, nobody can tap into your 2D messages, they exist in your hand, and you have the power to share them or keep them or destroy them, to cut them up or to stick them on your wall. You can save them for your kids some day, and you can guarantee that they will never have any ads added to them, they will never be updated or altered, never be challenged or spied on by any government or company. They're still fighting over the grid, but the 2Ds belong to us.

Fix your words, kiddo. Printing makes them yours.

A Life in Print
Lawrence Zeegen

For today's student artists and designers, who have grown up with a computer in the bedroom, playroom and classroom, using 'new technology' at art or design school isn't the big deal it once was a decade ago: these new Millennials have been the masters of digital kit for years. No, their 'new technology' is the traditional, the analogue, the real and the tangible. If you've never experienced letterpress, silk screen, etching or lithography before now, then this is your 'new technology'. As a digital native you're an analogue immigrant.

Stepping into a print studio is a very different experience from walking into a computer lab. First, it's the smell that hits you – don't worry, it's a good smell. It's the smell of print – the inks, the screens and plates, the paper, the machinery, the clean-up gear; it is a timeless smell, an evocative smell. It's the smell of Caxton's press, of Gutenberg's movable type; it's the smell of Warhol's Factory. It's the smell of industry. The whiff of the digital is the opposite: it's the whiff of screen-cleaner and of stale air, the scent of plastic, newness and corporations.

And then there is the sound of print. This is the sound of action, of machinery, of labour, of the here and now. You don't make prints quietly; you mix inks, you ink a plate, you pull a squeegee, you turn a wheel. These are physical acts and they are not silent; you hear metal on metal, you hear the sound of extraction fans, you hear the sound of activity; you engage with a mechanical process, you make it work for you. And with print you hear so much more than the tap, tap, tapping of fingers on keyboard and the electrical whirr of tiny fans.

Smell it, hear it, experience it: print is alive and well, and its much-expected demise following the explosion and expansion of the digital remains the headline that didn't deliver. Sure, print has become a more bespoke and artisan activity, much like vinyl is to download and, before that, CDs. Print has found a new life, a life not dependent on competing with the digital, a life existing with and without the digital, in tandem yet solo.

The resurgence and renewed interest in print wasn't an accident, but neither was it planned – most likely it was happenstance, the right conditions at the right time. A generation less than enamoured by the allure of the digital took to the plates and screens, presses and beds of yesterday with the passion to print for today and tomorrow. The Millennials, well used to gaming, texting, tweeting, posting and blogging, yearned for a real-world experience, and it was printmaking, physical and tangible, that gave young artists and designers an outlet.

The first time I stepped into a print studio was an experience I've never forgotten. I could smell it, hear it, breathe it, see it – here was a space and place where I could sense stuff happened. This was Camberwell School of Arts and Crafts in 1983 and I had arrived to commence a three-year BA (Hons) Graphic Arts degree. The print studios appeared to be inhabited by the rogues, rascals, rebels, renegades, rockers and the reprobates; here lived the radicals with attitude, with something to say and a medium to say it with. A mixed bunch of artists, graphic designers, illustrators, painters, photographers and printmakers: only the medium of print could bring together such a cross-disciplinary, cross-college cohort. Designing and printing record sleeves, gig posters, political placards, club flyers and T-shirts, this gang of ne'er-do-wells would typify many of the disparate groups forming around print studios and workshops in art schools across the country; post-punk, of course, but retaining enough attitude and angst to ensure that the 'do-it-yourself' culture would rock on.

These people of print in the early to mid-1980s simply wanted to get their messages out, wanted to inform, interrogate and irritate, and it was print, ahead of the digital revolution, that was the medium with the message. Getting straight to an audience was the key, but this was nothing new, of course. The 1960s had witnessed the birth of the psychedelic print. The LSD-fuelled hippy movement, born out of San Francisco, saw psychedelic art reign – 'Turn on, tune in, drop out' was the Timothy Leary call to inaction in 1966 and Haight-Ashbury was the scene's Mecca, a poster site for the prints expressing anger against the Vietnam War.

A decade later and it was the nihilism of punk in the 1970s that spawned a new graphic language of protest – from hastily silk-screen-printed posters promoting hastily created punk bands to the printed sloganeering of reborn Situationism, with Jamie Reid's 'Keep Warm This Winter – Make Trouble' and Dave King's graphics on protest placards for Rock Against Racism.

Fast-forward a decade or two, sidestepping the emergence of silk-screened paste-ups by street artists Faile across New York's Lower East Side and design duo Vault 49's attack on London's East End in the late 1990s and early 2000s, and arrive back into the recent past – the birth of the digital. 'Out with the old and in with the new' was the mantra as art and design schools, keen to embrace emerging technology, took out letterpress workshops and lithography set-ups to create bright new spaces for the digital hardware and software fast becoming the future.

But somehow a spark of the analogue remained alight; at first a few outposts kept a tradition alive, unfashionable Luddites on never-ending nostalgia trips holding a torch for an outmoded technology and a process destined for the scrapheap. As design went digital, like moths to a flame designers were drawn to the screen, yet there were those who kept the faith, kept true to an age-old medium where there is joy in the process, delight in the production. And it is because of those who believed in a world where silk screen could exist alongside touchscreen, where the real-world techniques of linocut, etching, monoprint and letterpress could live alongside the digital-world formats of TIFF, PDF and JPEG, that we have vital cottage industries keeping the creative industries alive with just the right balance of analogue and digital, for now at least.

Interview by Marcroy Smith

Interview: **Heretic**
Jon Rundall, Luke Frost and Therese Vandling

Tell us a little about Heretic – the company, your position, your role and your team . . .

Heretic consists of Jon Rundall, Luke Frost and Therese Vandling: we are a print/design/illustration studio based in Hackney, London. We work on independent projects, as well as taking on commissions. There is no hierarchy, we are all equals trying to work to our strengths depending on the type of project we are involved in.

How and when did Heretic start?

It happened quite organically; having all worked commercially we had the urge for more creative freedom and missed the tacticality of print. We all have a passion for printed work, so the studio came together in 2006 as a place to experiment with and to develop our screen printing and illustration practice. We have been collaborating and printing all together under the name Heretic from around 2008.

Wake up, go to the studio . . . there is no typical day. We all work very differently, we arrive at different times. There can be intense periods of print work, and intense periods of desk work. We like to sit down and eat lunch together.

Most of our work ends up being screen printed by us in our studio, especially self-initiated things. We also do various commissioned design jobs that may be printed in other ways depending on the scale of the job. Our studio is divided into two parts, a desk area and a print area.

Yes. Do what you enjoy, always experiment a lot, get things wrong, enjoy the mistakes, mishaps and glitches. Try not to be precious, embrace the uncertainty of outcome. Dream a lot. We always make sure to have lots of test prints on the go, we print layers of different prints on them, and this throws up unexpected combinations which in turn sparks ideas for future projects. Never give up. Smile at other people like you know them.

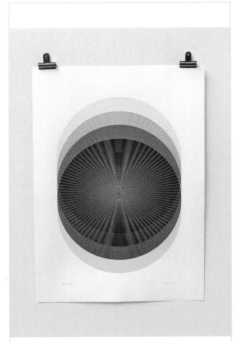

What or who are your biggest inspirations?

Everyone and everything around us. All the greats, Dieter Roth, Robert Rauschenberg, Bridget Riley, R. B. Kitaj, Eduardo Paolozzi, Roman Cieslewicz, Josef Albers.

What has been a favourite project you have worked on to date?

Each project we work on. We enjoy whatever we are doing right now. The installation we made at the Liverpool International Festival of Psychedelia last year was good fun. We collaborated with Sonic Boom, aka Peter Kember of Spacemen 3. We made an immersive print, sound and light installation, based around the idea of visual distortion, cuttlefish and dazzle ships. At the moment we are working on an ongoing, never-ending study into colour and the print process, a project called Spectral Nation.

Who are your favourite printers?

Seripop are so constant, we love what they are doing all the time.

What are the big plans for Heretic in the future?

We are working on some larger print works at the moment for an exhibition later this year. We have also just moved studio from our amazing home in Stoke Newington to Space Studios in Hackney. This was a pretty big deal as we had been in the same studio for seven or eight years. The move was mammoth – we are just recovering and getting used to our new space.

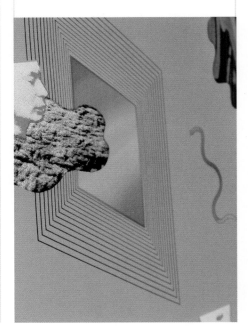

Luke: Piles of books for reference and collage. Four pairs of scissors, some glue, some pens, my arms, a rubber lizard that has been fashioned into a memory stick, a wooden elephant, a piece of coral from Florida, a long picture of Istanbul and lots of assorted cut-outs from books and magazines, three sketchbooks.

Jon: Lots of pens and pencils in jars and a box, books above me on a shelf, a Mexican flick knife in a leather pouch with a cockerel on it, quite a few offcuts of paper with things I don't want to forget written on them, soon to be lost. A sheet of paper with interesting word combinations. A Turkish man's holiday photos from the 1970s. My sketchbook. A bowl of small change.

Therese: I'd like to say that my desk is a place of minimal cleanliness but it's a constant battle and generally a war-zone of paper, pens, books, bits of paper that may be inspirational, to-do lists and general detritus. I also have a lot of plants, they are like little orphans that I have to look after and they are kind of taking over a bit, but I think they add a nice vibe to the studio. There is a cheeseplant named Marcel, a bunch of cactuses and succulents, and various types of ferns . . . just to mention a few.

St Cuthberts Mill
Marcroy Smith

We can print on to many things, including wood, metal and plastic, yet we must not forget an essential and staple material for our printing process: paper.

This year we had the privilege of visiting St Cuthberts Mill in Wells, Somerset, for a personal tour. The mill has been active since the 1700s and is the only mill in the UK that makes artist paper. Somerset paper is premium quality and is the buyer's choice for many printmakers across the globe. The mill is perfectly placed near the source of the River Axe, with its pure water filtered through the limestone of the Mendip Hills. Pure water is essential for creating quality paper; the trout swimming in the River Axe show that it is a perfect fresh-water source.

The first stage of papermaking at St Cuthberts Mill is the filtration of the water through large, historic sand filters. These clear any debris from the river water. Heavy rain means that more silt is brought into the system, affecting the production of the bright white paper that is so sought after by the artists who use this quality paper.

The filtered water gets pumped into a huge vat, or hydrapulper, along with 200 kg (440 lb) blocks of cotton linters, which is pulped into a porridge-like mixture called 'stuff'. The pulp is then pumped through wide tubes into large tiled containers known as 'stuff chests', and then on to the gigantic press. The stuff is collected on to a spinning cylinder complete with custom watermarks and fed by hand through a cylinder mould between two felts, giving the paper its signature texture. Each roller has two strips of paper in production at the same time, sectioned off by tape; this gives the paper its beautiful deckle edge.

The paper is dried to cure the sizing agent (which controls absorbency), then it is wetted again and dried again, this time being left to retain slight moisture. The paper is digitally measured to test that the weight is equal across the sheet before it comes off the press. Each batch of paper produced undergoes a series of strict control measures to make sure the paper is produced to the same standard every time.

1736

Handmade paper production starts on the St Cuthberts site under the name Lower Wookey Mill.

1899

Somerset watermark first used for writing paper.

1957

Current PM1 paper machine installed.

1981

Inveresk, including St Cuthberts Mill, is sold to Georgia Pacific and becomes GP Inveresk.

1999

Fine art inkjet papers developed and Somerset Enhanced launched.

Situated in the south-west of England, this historic paper mill has been making paper since the 1700s, taking advantage of the pure water of the River Axe. The mill is on the edge of the ancient cathedral city of Wells and is named after the local church dedicated to the seventh-century saint. The St Cuthbert's Cross illustrated on all the mill's artist papers is inspired by the cross on St Cuthbert's tomb in Durham Cathedral.

Nearly four hundred years ago papermaking started in the Axe Valley at Wookey Hole. It is now more than two hundred years – the date cannot be precise – since papermaking started on the St Cuthbert's site in Somerset. St Cuthberts Mill is the only surviving commercial paper mill out of the six once operating in the upper Axe Valley.

1835

First papermaking machine installed.

1907

Cylinder mould machine (still used to make artist papers) built.

1957

'Melamon' resin-loaded board first developed at Wookey Hole Mill.

1985

T. H. Saunders is developed to improve the surface strength of the paper and renamed Saunders Waterford.

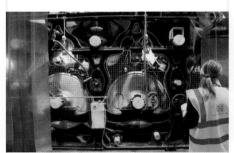

2002

Bockingford Inkjet launched.

1850

Present frontage of the mill is built using local stone.

1927

St Cuthberts Mill becomes a major shareholder in Scottish paper manufacturer Inveresk.

1959

Wookey Hole purchases the rights to produce T. H. Saunders paper (originally developed in 1920).

1990

Inveresk is sold by Georgia Pacific to the Inveresk management in a management buyout.

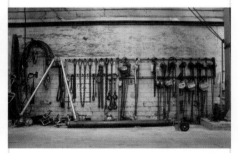

2007

Somerset Photo launched.

1862

The mill is renamed Mendip Mill, in honour of the local hills.

1887

The mill is renamed again as St Cuthberts Mill, after the parish of the local church in which it is situated.

1897

Office building built.

1931

St Cuthberts Mill is bought by Inveresk.

1950

Inveresk buys nearby Wookey Hole Mill (first established in 1425).

1952

Cylinder mould machine installed at Wookey Hole.

1972

Wookey Hole Mill sold (now a tourist attraction) and the mould machine transferred to St Cuthberts Mill. Watercolour paper production now solely made at St Cuthberts Mill (including handmade, which will continue until 1976).

1975

Bockingford rights purchased from Whatman.

1976

Somerset traditional printmaking paper developed and launched.

1991

£3 million investment in PM1 for pre-impregnated decorative papers.

1993

Inveresk floated on the Stock Exchange.

1994

Somerset Velvet Radiant White developed and launched, creating an uncoated inkjet paper without the dot gain associated with uncoated papers.

2010

St Cuthberts Mill Ltd created.

Interview by Marcroy Smith

Interview: **magCulture**
Jeremy Leslie

What was the biggest motivation that made you launch magCulture? Any particular magazines that inspired you at the time?

The magCulture site was first launched in 2004 with the intention of using it as a source for updates to my 2003 book *magCulture*. The CMS [content management system] I was using was so awkward the site was essentially dormant for two years, but then I became curious about blogging and I moved the site over to WordPress in February 2006. And the experiment just took off – it was easy to post material, and it was exactly the time that editorial designers were discovering the Web as a source of inspiration, and publishers were installing broadband links. So I quickly had an audience and the site grew from there.

The magazines that inspired me to make the book and site originally were those I collected when travelling – the early wave of the current independents. The industry was far less international, you could visit a European capital and find magazines you'd never heard of – *032c* when it was still a newspaper, *Re-*, and

in the US, *Speak* and *Nest*. That said, the very first post on magCulture was about *Grazia*, a design favourite of mine though a thoroughly mainstream mag (sadly it was one of the victims of data loss during a random hack last year).

Can you give us some titles that you think have made a big impact on the magazine industry over the past twenty-five years?

That goes back to the start of my career in magazines: the original style mags *The Face*, *i-D* and *Blitz* (where I was art director). They catalysed the industry, and led the way for what we know as print magazines today. Since then? Too many to mention them all, but off the top of my head highlights would include early *Little White Lies* – inspiration for so many indie mags; *Kasino A4* for its crazy attitude to how a magazine can be edited; *Colors* for the way it foresaw globalization and the Internet; *Carlos* for moving beyond the assumption that a magazine had to be about photography and full-colour; *Fantastic Man* for matching text and design so perfectly; *Bloomberg Businessweek* for reasserting the idea that the mainstream could be challenging.

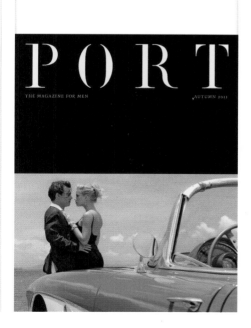

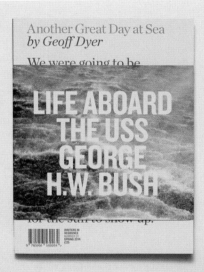

Besides seeking to survive the digitization of publishing, is there anything else you are looking for in print magazines? What have you not seen in the print magazine industry and what would you like see – in terms of both the design and the contents?

There's this idea that a new big idea or niche is always just around the corner; actually, the tough part is executing that idea well and in a manner that engages people. That counts for digital publishing too. It's all about quality. I'm pro-print, but also pro-digital. I'm interested to see examples of the two working together to produce great writing and images that benefit from intelligent design.

What has been the most exciting experience in your career?

The most significant thing was the Colophon conferences, held in Luxembourg. Mike Koedinger, Andrew Losowsky and I co-curated two of these three-day celebrations of independent magazines, in 2007 and 2009. I remember arriving at the venue for the first Colophon quite unsure whether the whole thing was going to work. But it surpassed all expectations, there was genuine excitement about people coming together to share the experience of making magazines. There was a shared, almost visceral excitement in the air. The ripples from Colophon continue through my practice and through independent publishing today.

The challenge is keeping all the parts going – the design studio, the blog and associated writing projects, responding to interviews like this, speaking at conferences and organizing our own events (I do Printout [independent magazine talks] every two months with Steve Watson plus two annual day-long events, one in Munich and one in London). Different parts of the brain get used for the various activities.

You seem to be working with different projects all the time, a lot of collaborations, and you also work for yourself — what are the secrets to balancing all sides of your practice?

I've worked for large companies and I know the pressures they exert in terms of having to do things you don't want to do. I value independence enormously, and the pay-off for the relative lack of financial security is you can be selective about what you do, and strong about what you don't do.

I enjoy the many sides of what I do, but they do all inform each other.

MY FAV O (U) RI TE MAG AZINE

*Are there any projects that we should
be expecting to see from magCulture in
the near future?*

Plenty. Another editorial design conference late summer in London, and a collaboration with one of my favourite furniture brands, as part of London Design Festival; a revitalized online magazine shop; a new magazine project about to crowdsource funding; and later this year the first fruits of my creative director role with [independent publisher] Maison Moderne.

*And, last question, any sage tips for those
who want to start up a print magazine?*

I've developed the habit of first saying 'Don't' to anyone who asks. Then if the person persists I'll quietly encourage them. A magazine is like letting a really needy new friend into your life. It'll piss off all your existing friends, spouses, partners. Prepare yourself for that, then make sure you do it your way.

Be independent.

THE MODERN MAGAZINE

VISUAL JOURNALISM IN THE DIGITAL ERA

JEREMY LESLIE

Part 2: Features

[1] Lollipop Queen, digital, 2014

Age of Reason

Illustration, design
Hove, UK

Age of Reason is a UK print label with a playful punk twist. It prides itself on making beautiful natural-fibre scarves from silk, cashmere and wool, which are available in some of the world's best boutiques. Audacious prints and beautiful fabrics define the work, which is inspired by the collision between designer Ali Mapletoft's African childhood and the streets of London. Ali marries her own sketchy drawing style with bold colour combinations and textures inspired by her travel and personal history.

A large dose of quintessentially British humour finishes off Ali's signature style.

'I want Age of Reason to be the antidote to cute kitten and chintzy flowers on scarves,' says Ali. 'My passion is to surprise and delight people by creating things that are more thoughtful, bolder, naughtier or more exciting than expected. A scarf should never be boring, it should become part of your own style story and be a very special rare thing that can't be found everywhere.'

[3] Age of Reason permanent collection classic scarves, digital, 2014
(overleaf)

[1] Creative Opportunities in Architecture, offset, 2013

[2] FPCEUP Calendars, offset, 2011—2014

And Atelier

Graphic design
Porto, Portugal

And Atelier is a small independent design studio founded in 2010 by João Araújo and Rita Huet and currently based in Porto, Portugal. Working as a duo, Araújo and Huet love to be involved in every step of the project and to control every detail, working closely with clients, collaborators and friends, in order to meet everyone's expectations and dreams. The studio has mainly focused on editorial and poster design propjects, but has also recently begun to develop exhibition spaces, starting at the International Poster and Graphic Design Festival of Chaumont, France (2012), and three-dimensional installations (EXD '13 Biennale, Lisbon). Their work always tries to accomplish a strong conceptual approach, through very clean solutions and with a strong typographic component and respect for letterforms and reading rhythms. Above all, the duo try to do something they believe in. In order to get there, there is a whole process of research into ways that make sense and that they can defend and justify, both to themselves and to others. This process is always characterized by uncertainty, either about what the final object will be or about following the best possible route. They seek to discuss everything together, trying to understand the project's context and boundaries. For them, having two different views always present is one way to ensure objectivity, because sometimes they are so absorbed that it is difficult to have the necessary distance to make certain decisions.

[4] *Dédalo* #7 magazine, offset, 2010
(overleaf)

CASA
DAS ARTES

RUA DE RUBEN A
Nº 210, PORTO

MINÁRIO
NTERNACIONAL

A CIDADE
SGATAD

AR

[5] Iberia Critica – Young Portuguese and Spanish Architects in Debate, offset, 2013

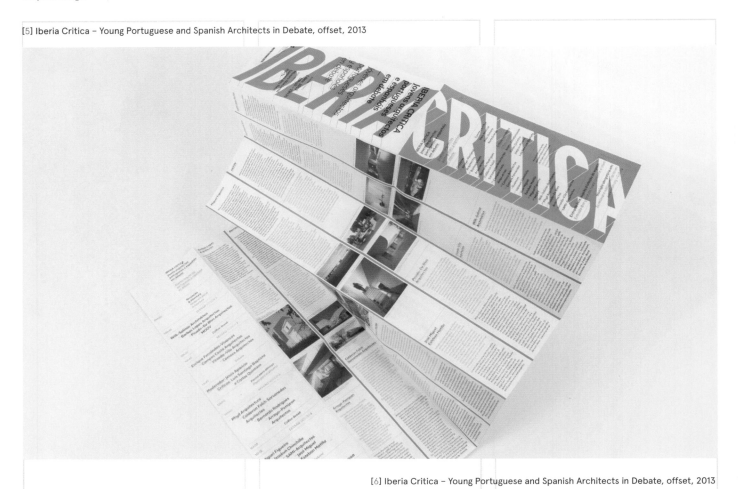

[6] Iberia Critica – Young Portuguese and Spanish Architects in Debate, offset, 2013

[1] North & South Ampersand, woodblock, 2013

[2] Work Hard & Be Nice To People, woodblock, 2004

WORK
HARD
&
BE NICE
TO PEOPLE

Anthony Burrill

Graphic art, printmaking
London, UK

Graphic artist, printmaker and designer Anthony Burrill is known for his persuasive, upbeat style of communication. His work is held in the permanent collections of the Victoria and Albert Museum in London and the Cooper-Hewitt National Design Museum in New York, and has been exhibited in galleries around the world, including the Barbican, London, the Walker Art Center, Minneapolis, and the Graphic Design Museum, Breda. In 2012, he made his first foray into curating with the exhibition 'Made in L.A.' at KK Outlet in London. Words and language are an important part of Burrill's output and he has developed a distinctive voice that is sought after not only by collectors of his posters and prints but also by clients including *Wallpaper**, *The Economist*, the British Council, London Underground and the Design Museum, London. Burrill is perhaps best known for his typographic, text-based compositions, including the now-famous 'Work Hard & Be Nice to People', which has become a mantra for the design community and beyond. Burrill has a long-standing relationship with the printers Adams of Rye, where he uses traditional techniques to compose and print his work. The integrity lent to the process of image-making by handmade methods is essential to his practice across all media — from print to screen-based to three-dimensional applications. In 2010 he worked with Happiness Brussels to design a screen-printed poster made with oil.

YOU KNOW MORE THAN YOU THINK YOU DO

Anthony Burrill for the RSA

ASK
QUES

MORE
TIONS

SWERS

ill

[5] Wood type from the collection at Adams of Rye, East Sussex, UK

[6] Think Of Your Own Ideas, woodblock, 2009

[7] I Like It. What Is It?, woodblock, 2010

[8] Wood type from the collection at Adams of Rye, East Sussex, UK

[9] Spread from I Like It. What Is It?, offset, 2013

[10] Spread from I Like It. What Is It?, offset, 2013

Think About All You Say
2012

Burrill has worked on several projects with the British Council around the world. In 2009 he was one of six designers invited to participate in Timeless, the British Council's contribution to that year's ExperimentaDesign Lisboa cultural biennale staged in the Portuguese city.

Participating designers were asked to create a piece of work specific to Lisbon. Mirroring his relationship with Adams of Rye, Burrill planned to work with a printer in Lisbon that was still using wood and metal type.

A research trip to the city proved unsuccessful, but, in a signmaker's shop, Burrill found a set of cut metal stencils of individual letters and decided to use those instead for his project. The set of four posters feature a typical local phrase, 'Think about all you say – do not say all you think about', in both English and Portuguese.

1 The original metal stencils
  used to make Burrill's posters

2 The posters were pasted on
  walls throughout the Bairro
  Alto district of Lisbon

[1] Secret 7" Karmacoma, digital, 2014

Ben Rider

Graphic design, printmaking, illustration
London, UK

Ben Rider is a fluorescent-ink-obsessed print mercenary based in London. An enthusiastic image maker, he loves the energy and potential for experimentation of printmaking. A commercial illustrator and teacher, he dives into self-initiated projects when time allows. Ben's clients have included the Victoria and Albert Museum, University of the Arts London, Brew Dog, O2 Ireland and Samsung, and he produces work for independent magazines and studios in London and internationally.

Ben's work can be described as punky, vibrant and bursting with energy, built up from a dense hybrid of drawings and collaged imagery, utilizing a love for the offsets, fades, drips and all those happy accidents and small imperfections found within printmaking and working with your hands. His signature is a calm chaos of experimentation, combining different processes, multiple layers, mixed media, even found material or household cleaning products, into a single print, favouring stylistic expression

over precision and cleanliness. Ben works in conjunction with the print process, almost creating a collaboration between himself and the process. His prints are one of a kind (more often than not literally) and his work rate unstoppable.

Although vibrant and playful by nature, his work often hides a more serious tone and content below the surface. His education background in Design for Graphic Communication at London College of Communication taught him the value of research

[3] Sticker Pack, screen print, 2014
(overleaf)

[4] Greed, screen print / collage, 2013

[5] Lust, screen print / collage, 2013

[6] Cyanotype Test 1, cyanotype / screen print, 2013

[7] Cyanotype Test 2, cyanotype / screen print, 2013

[8] False Gods, screen print, 2014

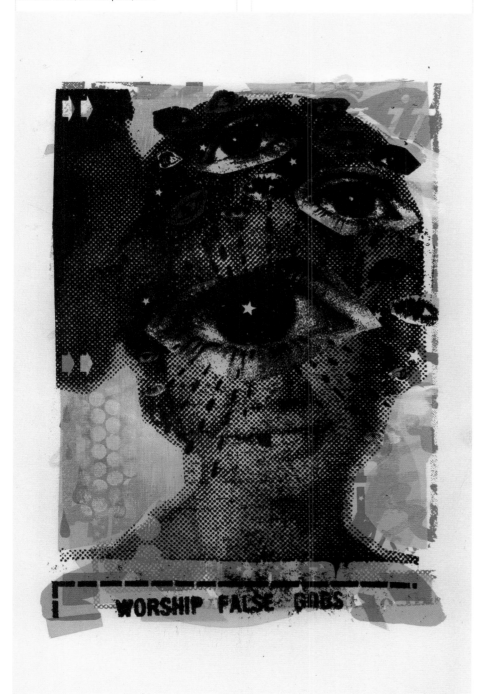

and the use of this as a basis to create work with content. For example, a female police officer beholding a dildo may at first glance appear silly or offensive, but at a deeper level reveals themes of lust and the objectification of others for personal gain. This subtext of varying content is central to both his commercial and his personal work.

Ben loves the gratifying nature of print and what it can add to an illustration. The sense of physically making something with your hands has an honesty, giving work a certain soul and character, and to him this acts as a middle finger to the increasingly homogenized and slick corporate world sold to us.

[1] Fruithead, screen print, 2012

[2] Go Skate, screen print, 2011

Bicicleta Sem Freio

Illustration
Goiânia, Goiás, Brazil

Art, design and rock 'n' roll. It might sound like a cliché, but this is the simplest, most honest and coherent way of trying to explain this power trio of Brazilian illustrators who answer to the name of Bicicleta Sem Freio ('Bicycle Without Brakes'). Douglas de Castro, Victor Rocha and Renato Reno met on the Visual Arts course at the Federal University of Goiás. The BSF came together as a big group of class colleagues who just wanted to have fun, create, draw and animate whatever came into their minds. Most of the early work comprised posters for rock concerts and cultural events. (In a way this experience would directly influence the birth of the band Black Drawing Chalks – of the three, only Renato isn't in the band.)

The main characteristics of this group are the manual work, the care with the typography and the drawing of girls, a lot of girls. With influences that go from Edward Mucha to James Jean, the boys explore in a masterly way the colours, shapes and curves of a variety of girls, always with a dose of unique psychedelic humour.

It perhaps wouldn't be exaggerating to say that they live what they draw. Sometimes that doesn't quite work, but most of the time the result is astounding and genius. The team effort has raised awareness on all continents, with the group lending their unique touch to customers around the world – not bad for three boys riding a bike at full speed without any kind of brakes.

[4] Wolf, screen print, 2013
(overleaf)

[7] Go Skate, screen print, 2011

[6] Fruithead, screen print, 2012

[1] DESO — DOD, screen print, 2013

[2] DESO — HABSORA, screen print, 2013

Broken Fingaz Crew

Illustration
Haifa, Israel

Founded in 2001, multidisciplinary art collective Broken Fingaz (Kip, Unga, Tant and Deso) are regarded as one of the first graffiti crews to emerge from Haifa, Israel, and their name is now at the forefront of contemporary street art. With their independent approach and shared appreciation of illustration, the BFC's success has been unprecedented on the international scene. In more than a decade of working together, they are renowned for their unique style, inspired by the

peaks and troughs of life, everyday ephemera, old comic books, 1980s skateboards graphics, and neo-psychedelia, among many other things. They started out painting on the street and designing posters and graphics for local venues, but the BFC's work now encompasses graphic design, painting, film and installation. Underlining the importance of their contributions to the shape of the contemporary scene, their work has been presented at exhibitions at Israel's most important

visual arts institutes, the Tel Aviv Museum (2011) and the Haifa Museum of Art (2010). Since then they have exhibited widely outside Israel: in 2012 they presented their debut international solo exhibition in London (Old Truman Brewery, 2012), with shows following in Vienna (Inoperable, 2012), Paris (Lebenson Gallery, 2012), Amsterdam (Battalion Gallery, 2013) and Berlin (Urban Spree, 2013). In 2013 they were also invited to participate at Cut Out Festival, Queretaro, Mexico, where they produced a

[4] UNGA — HAMAM 3, screen print, 2013
(overleaf)

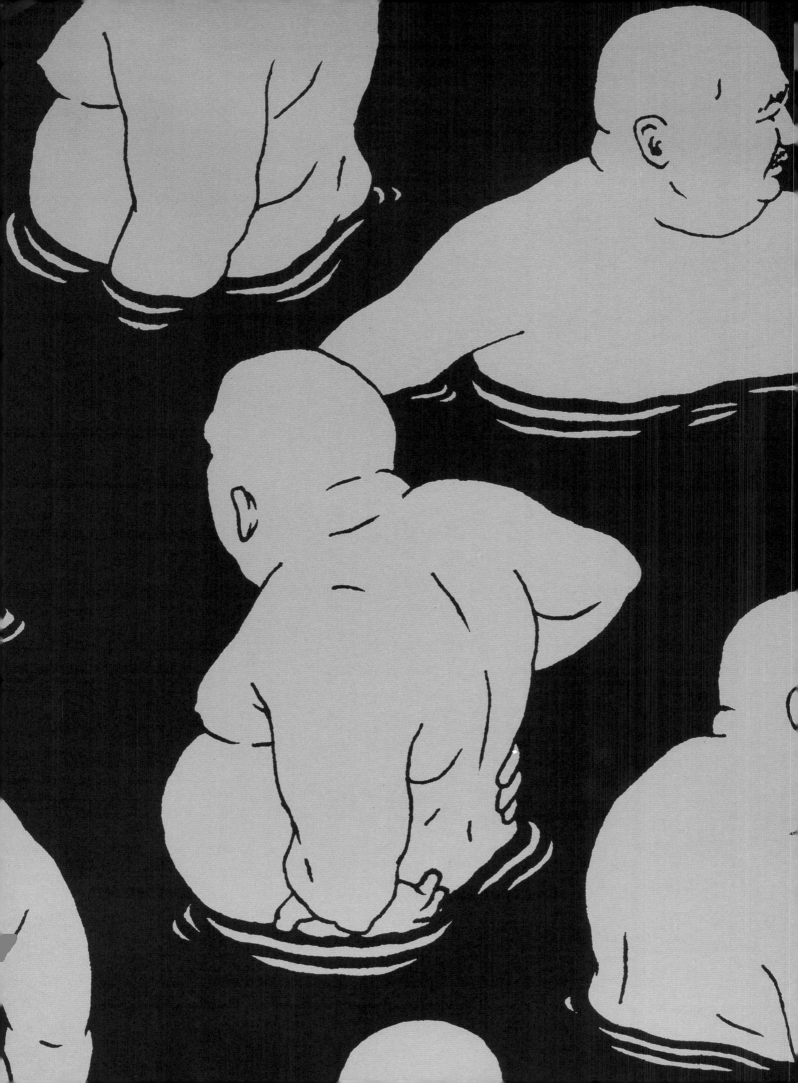

[6] UNGA — Dead Dancers, screen print, 2013

[7] UNGA — Red Dancers, screen print, 2013

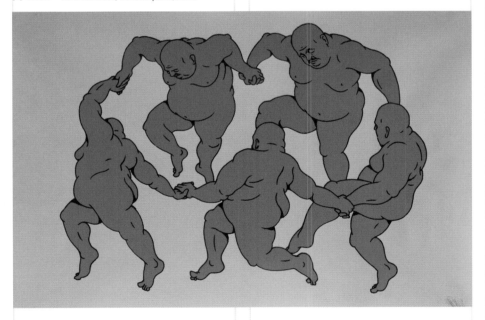

new stop-motion graffiti film. Their public murals can be seen on the streets of cities across China, Japan, Cambodia, Israel, the UK, Germany, Holland, Italy, Austria, Switzerland, France, Spain, Mexico and more. In the press, the crew are regularly featured in art magazines, including *Juxtapoz*, *Complex* and *VNA*.

[1] Build – Works (01), litho, 2013 (reprint)

−092

Build

Graphic design
London, UK

Founded in 2001, Build is a boutique creative agency based in London, producing modern graphic solutions for lifestyle clients, both corporate and independent. Clients include Getty Images, Nokia, Made.com, Sony Music and the Design Museum, London.

Build specializes in producing visual identities and communications for design-led clients. Its portfolio encompasses brand identity, art direction and graphic design, with extensive experience of production including print, websites and moving image. The studio's core strengths are showcased in a portfolio unified by a strong and confident visual language. Its work has been published in more than 100 books and magazines around the world.

[4] Timothy Saccenti Portraits (01), litho, 2014

[5] Timothy Saccenti Portraits (01), litho, 2014

[6] Generation Press stationery set, 2013–2014

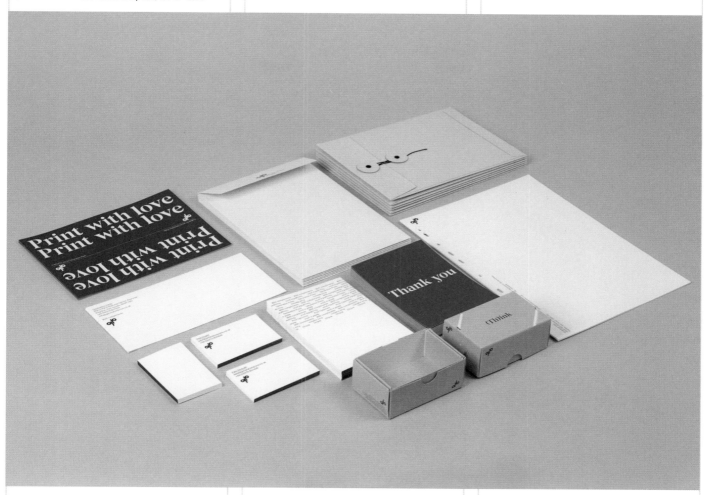

[7] Build stationery set, letterpress, 2012

[1] Animalia No. 2 Black, digital, 2012

[2] Animalia No. 2 Black, digital, 2012

[3] Animalia No. 2 Black, digital, 2012

[4] Animalia No. 2 Black, digital, 2012

Carnovsky

Graphic design
Milan, Italy

Carnovsky are a Milan-based art/design duo comprising Silvia Quintanilla and Francesco Rugi. They work on the threshold between art and design, mixing different worlds, disciplines and techniques, such as using wallpaper to create frescoes that continuously mutate via interaction with coloured lights ('RGB'), or creating architectures through purses ('Artificialia'). Colour is a key issue in their work, so they are always experimenting with different processes and techniques to arrive at the right colours when printing on various materials, whether it is to create wallpaper, limited-edition prints, garments, accessories or furniture, or utilizing hand-dyed fibres for carpets and tapestry. The use of wallpaper as a sort of contemporary fresco in combination with RGB (red-green-blue) colour-changing lights allows Carnovsky to create completely immersive environments in which the viewer acts like an explorer in an ever-changing world. Their limited editions, ranging from prints to large screens and tapestry, enable them to work on the richness of the materials and to use traditional techniques in creating a unique piece. The general theme of their work is metamorphosis, narrating a story of the elements pictured through the idea of their unceasing mutation and transformation. Carnovsky's visual universe, inspired by their fascination for antique natural-history books and reproduction techniques such as engraving, with its richness of stroke, is populated by real and imaginary

[7] Jungla No. 1 Black, digital, 2011

[8] Vesalio Screen, UV ink / digital, 2012

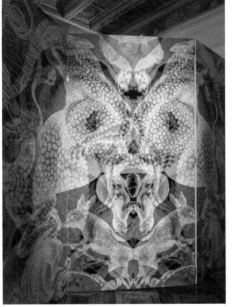

[9] Vesalio Carpet, hand-knotted rug, 196 knots/inch, 2011

creatures, plants, anatomical studies, landscapes, gods, atmospheric phenomena and so on.

Carnovsky use reproductions of original engravings, mostly from the eighteenth and nineteenth centuries. They prefer this period because they like to think of each animal, plant or object as a sort of character in an immense narrative, and these original images, with their subtle balance between the realistic and the fantastical, have a certain look or mood as if they are trying to say something, which is important in the conception of their work. In fact, there is a mix of old and new in Carnovsky's work, so that it is hard to position it in history. On the one hand their imaginative stimulus comes from ancient sources, though the output is quite contemporary; on the other they are always experimenting with new technologies in printing, production and lighting. In the end, their work deals with history, memories, the recreational and even childish part in everyone, creating an emotional tie that is what remains in people's memory.

[1] Love Cats, screen print, 2012

Corrupiola

Illustration
São José, Brazil

Leila Lampe and Aleph Ozuas are designers and crafters who love cats and printing and who run Corrupiola 'handmade experiences' together from São José, in the south of Brazil. They work with paper, inks, fabrics, vintage maps and comics to produce beautiful handmade stationery, in particular little notebooks that they call Corrupios (*corrupio* is Portuguese for 'fun').

Leila and Aleph were both designers before they met in 1999. Leila graduated in Fine Arts and

before that had learned the crafts of knitting and embroidery from her mother. Writer and web designer Aleph studied Engineering and Systems Analysis followed by English Literature at university. Influenced by his father's skills as well as by his own mix of interests, he believes that our hands are the most amazing tools on earth, capable of doing everything we want.

At the beginning, they spent almost two years getting ready to do their first print, cleaning and

fixing machines and collecting old fonts and print blocks. All their products are handmade one unit at a time, using no industrial manufacturing processes or cheap labour. The Corrupios, their main product, are stitched by hand, using high-quality acid-free papers.

Once inspiration has struck they usually take some time to think about the idea before putting it into practice – sketching their ideas in their own Corrupio notebooks. They discuss the concept

[3] Corrupio AQUI?, letterpress, 2012

[4] Corrupio AQUI?, letterpress, 2012

of each material and how they want the finished product to be. Sometimes they transfer their ideas to computer: with silk screen, for example, ideas are always worked out on the computer first, although the process begins almost every time in a notebook, as an idea or a sketch.

The duo are planning new notebooks with different formats and materials, and they also make stationery cards, with the aim of diversifying and offering more than notebooks. They say that to them, their previous work was always the most interesting, but they confess that they almost cried when they saw their first letterpress notebook finished.

[5] Corrupio AQUI?, letterpress, 2012

[6] Corrupio AQUI?, letterpress, 2012

[9] The Most Flexible Way box, screen print, 2013

[8] The Most Flexible Way box, screen print, 2013

[1] Dangerfork silk screen, 2013,

[2] Megan and Chris, 2013,
interview for *The Opening Hours*

[3] Ink dots black spots, 2013

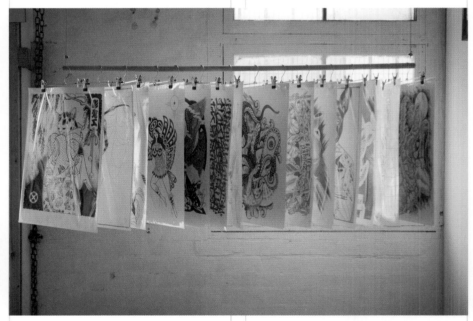

Dangerfork

Printmaking
Melbourne, Australia

Dangerfork, the brainchild of creative couple Chris Drummond and Megan Quigley, produces and sells limited-edition screen prints. The Melbourne-based boutique screen printer and print gallery, where these artists print work for other artists, was born in 2010, when the husband-and-wife team returned to their home city after a stint in Europe.

Specializing in fine-art screen printing, Chris and Megan print on a number of media including wood, canvas, glass and film, but favour paper printing. They endeavour to maintain the highest level of quality and workmanship by collaborating with each artist to produce the best possible screen print. They often work with each artist personally to help establish a basic understanding of screen printing and highlight the qualities the medium can bring to the artwork.

Dangerfork uses a hand-pulled screen-printing process, and prints using environmentally friendly water-based inks. Because everything is done by hand there are many variables that can have an impact on the final product, but that's simply part of the charm of screen printing. Every print is unique and is numbered and embossed with the Dangerfork seal. Dangerfork sells a selection of limited-edition prints by Australian and international artists through its studio space in Melbourne.

[5] Chris Drummond's hands, 2013 (overleaf)

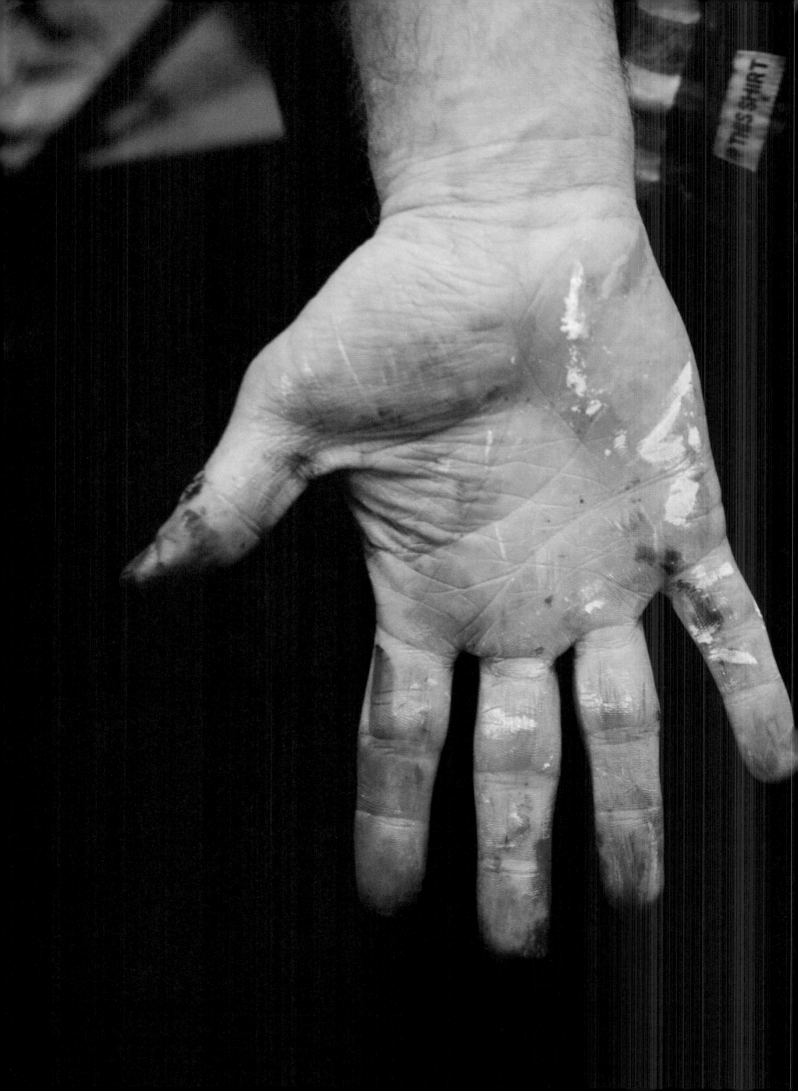

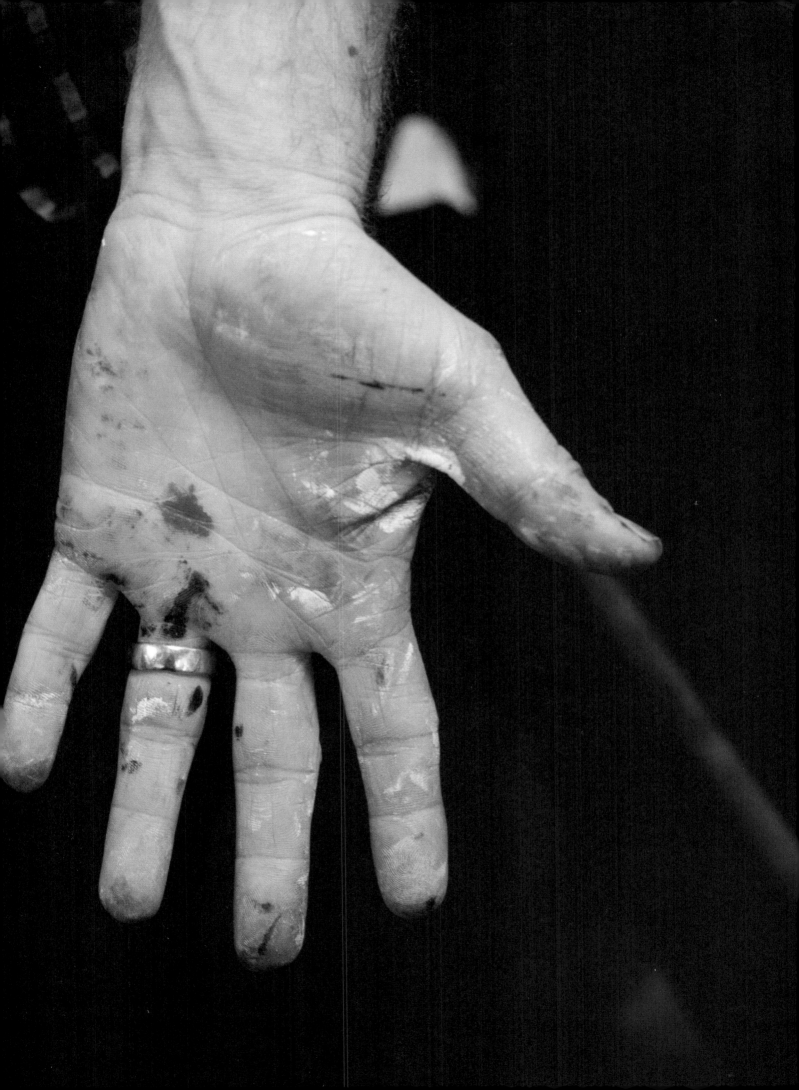

[6] Mysterious Al print on racks, 2012

[7] Colour swatches, 2013

[8] Test prints, 2013

Dolly Demoratti

Printmaking
Berlin, Germany

Sometime in 2010, a small independent silk-screen print house appeared in a modest shop space in the quiet district of Kreuzberg in Berlin. Named Mother Drucker, the studio-cum-gallery space was put together by two English expats, Dolly Demoratti and Gemma Brewer. The name 'Drucker' is a play on words, though it leaves non-German-speaking people guessing. Simply, *Drucker* is the German word for printer.

Dolly originally moved to Berlin from London looking for a print studio to continue her career as a silk-screen printer. In terms of finding a working space open to anyone, especially one set up at a professional level, this proved difficult. What she found instead were closed doors, or studios with a DIY set-up. It seemed clear that in contrast to London, here the high-end silk-screen printing scene was limited. So Mother Drucker was set up,

specializing mostly in high-quality silk-screen print on paper, creating editions with artists from around the world, as well as producing professionally on a commission basis. Since then Dolly has gained a respected clientele list and worked with top names in the art industry. To further unite with her fellow printmakers and enthusiasts, Dolly staged Berlin's first-ever festival of print, Druck Berlin, in August 2011. A constant and eclectic stream of live print

sessions, tutorials and workshops over two days, the festival fulfilled its goal of acting as a platform for learning and involvement for anyone with any level of interest. The second Druck Berlin took place in December 2013 over three weekends, connecting people from all over the world with a mutual interest in print, art and design. Having tripled in size since the first, attracting thousands of visitors and countless printers, Druck Berlin is now set to become the largest print festival of its kind in future years.

During the spring of 2012 and by then working alone, Dolly moved Mother Drucker to a new location in Berlin to join forces with art and music venue Urban Spree. To celebrate the collaboration Dolly invited designer Christoph Reichert to join her in hosting Urban Spree's first exhibition in the newly acquired and completely unrenovated 400 sq m (4300 sq ft) gallery space. The show, 'Grand Boucle', displayed printed materials oriented around vintage bicycle design. Following its popularity in Berlin, the exhibition toured throughout the next year to Budapest and London.

Mother Drucker is committed to curating and holding print-oriented exhibitions and events in Berlin and beyond. In 2014 a new venture saw Mother Drucker expanding its services to include an open studio. The studio has a professional set-up, and can be hired by artists and printers practising at any level. So what Dolly was looking to find for herself when she first landed in Berlin, she now provides for others. She has Mother Drucker and the art of screen printing well and truly stamped on the Berlin map, and has helped to establish the city as a print focus of global significance.

[1] 'Album Beauty', installation, Foam (Fotografiemuseum Amsterdam), 2012

[2] KesselsKramer installation, Triennale Design Museum, Milan, 2012

Erik Kessels

Graphic design
Amsterdam, The Netherlands

Erik Kessels has been creative director of communications agency KesselsKramer in Amsterdam since 1996 and works for national and international clients. He has a background in graphic design and with his daily practice in KesselsKramer is involved in many print executions as part of campaigns.

As both an artist and a photography collector Kessels has published about fifty books of his 'collected' images, including *Missing Links* (1999), *The Instant Men* (2000), *in almost every picture* (2001–14)

and *Wonder* (2006). Since 2000, he has been an editor of the alternative photography magazine *Useful Photography*.

Kessels has exhibited in and curated exhibitions such as 'Loving Your Pictures' (2006), 'The European Championship of Graphic Design' (2008), 'Use me Abuse me' (2010), 'Graphic Detour' (2011–12), 'Album Beauty' (2012) and '24 HRS of Photos' (2012). For this last project Kessels downloaded twenty-four hours' worth of photographs from Flickr, printed

them and overloaded a gallery space with them. For an exhibition in the Victoria and Albert Museum in London in 2013, Kessels made a huge 'Memory Palace' out of recycled papers and letters. By walking through, people could read the installation.

In 2010 Kessels was awarded the Amsterdam Prize of the Arts and in 2012 he was elected as the most influential creative of the Netherlands. In 2014 an overview of Kessels's work was shown at the gallery Pier 24 Photography in San Francisco.

[4] '24 HRS of Photos', installation, Foam (Fotografiemuseum Amsterdam), 2012 (overleaf)

At the height of the Booming,
sign was so plentiful that it

fell   from   like
         the
         sky   rain.

It rustled underfoot in autumn
and rose and fluttered about
the palaces and hospitals
like apple blossom in spring.

as called Advertising

On a deep crack in the wor
I put a spell or essay by a n
known as the Pope. It is an
to dominate the world with

Go wander creature where sign guides,

Go measure earth

[5] KesselsKramer installation, Triennale Design Museum, Milan, 2012

[6] KesselsKramer installation, Triennale Design Museum, Milan, 2012

[1] Untitled, screen print, 2012

[2] Untitled, screen print, 2012

Fatherless

Graphic design, illustration, printmaking
Barcelona, Spain

Fatherless is a collective of artists, printmakers, designers, educators and graffiti writers, started as a venture between Corey Hagberg, Jarrod Hennis, Javier Jimenez and Greg Lang in the spring of 2010. Initially they planned seasonal shows in which they created screen prints together, live, during the event. When an idea came about to feature a guest artist for a series, they chose a local artist and instructor of printmaking to work with, and it was a natural fit. Dave Menard became a full-time member following that show.

Their influences are many and are certainly captured by what they have termed a 'Rust Belt Power Pop' aesthetic. Their finished pieces aim to mirror the sense of chaos and detachment that is communicated in the current consumer-driven social climate. A good portion of their imagery is recontextualized from current throwaway culture to create a finished piece.

The name 'Fatherless' was decided upon based on the notion that each member, although responsible for bringing individual styles and

influences to the table, would work on each and every print made, but through a process that may lead to working independently with each other's images. All prints have been worked at some point by each artist in the group. They are not five artists that work 'under' the name of Fatherless. A Fatherless print is made by five artists.

[4] Untitled, screen print, 2013

[5] Untitled, screen print, 2013

[6] Untitled, screen print, 2012

[7] Untitled, screen print, 2014

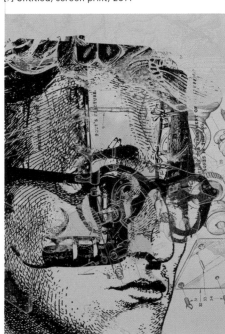

[8] Untitled, screen print, 2013

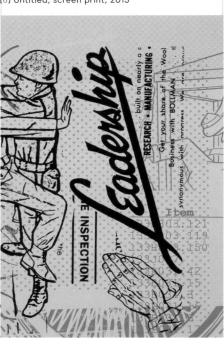

[9] Untitled, screen print, 2014

[10] Untitled, screen print, 2013

[11] Untitled, screen print, 2013

[12] Untitled, screen print, 2014

[13] Untitled, screen print, 2012

[14] Untitled, screen print, 2014

[15] Untitled, screen print, 2014

[17] Untitled, screen print, 2014

[16] Untitled, screen print, 2013

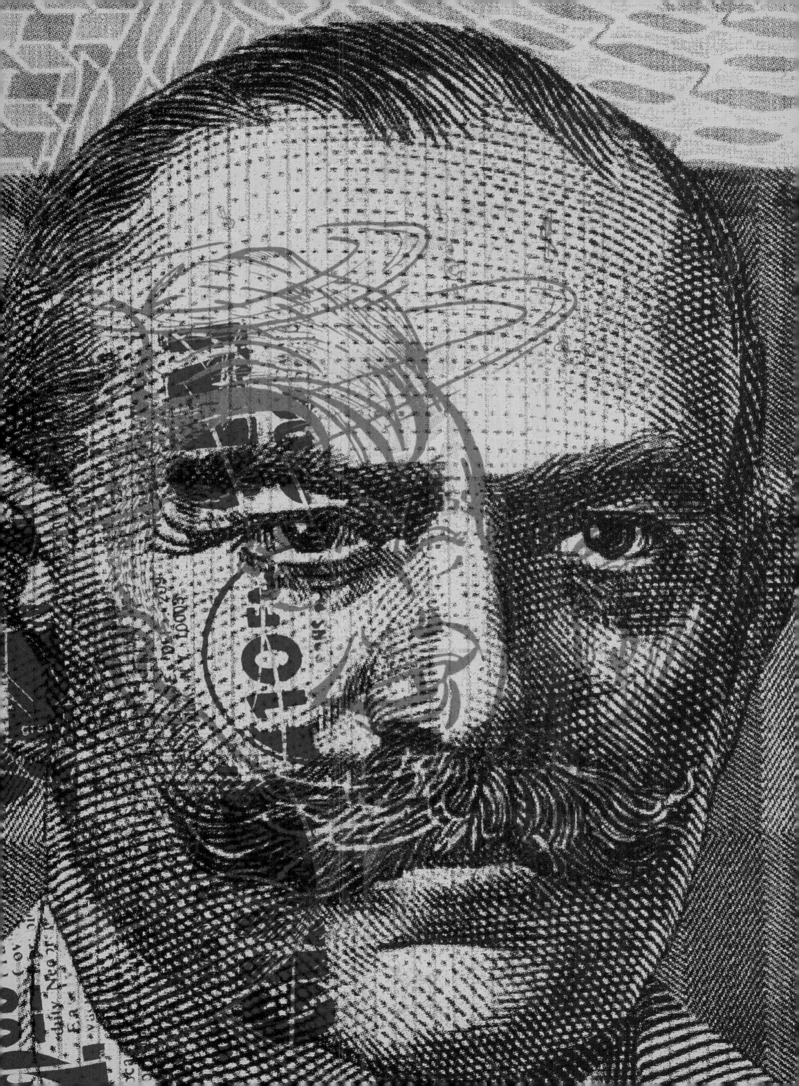

[1] Jon Arne Berg and Frode Skaren, screen print, 2014

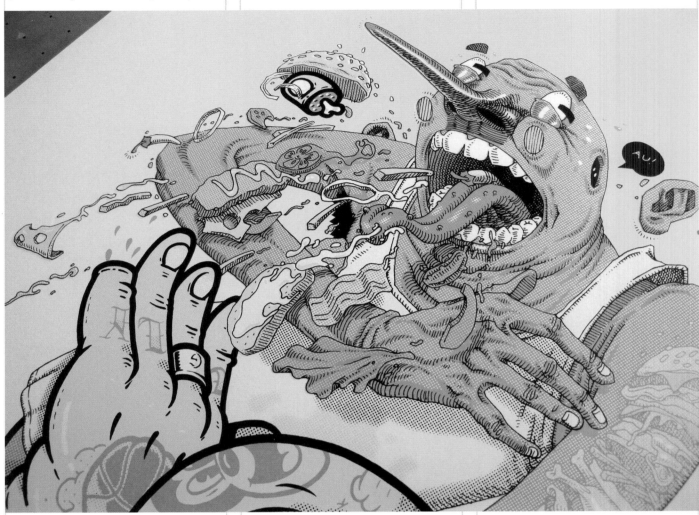

Fellesverkstedet

Illustration
Oslo, Norway

Fellesverkstedet (The Shared Workshop) is a production space that builds bridges between ideas and production. Based in Oslo, Norway, the workshop creates a stable foundation that allows creative people to use their own hands to make almost anything. It's a simple concept: people who make things need an infrastructure to get their ideas out into the world. Fellesverkstedet offers large-scale production facilities, equipment and machinery, assistance and courses – all under the same roof, in an old steel factory right in the middle of the city. Subsidized by Arts Council Norway and the local municipality, Fellesverkstedet is able to make its facilities available to everyone.

The printing facilities at Fellesverkstedet are based around traditional workshops for screen print and letterpress. The majority of the equipment has been collected, inherited or purchased from old printing houses and schools at a time when traditional print production is constantly being replaced by automatic presses and copy machines. Fellesverkstedet breathes new life into this old equipment, and adapts these historical printing techniques to the demands of today's and tomorrow's artists, designers and innovators. In addition to this, Fellesverkstedet is always pushing forwards and challenging the boundaries of print by combining these analogue techniques with digital tools: old machinery and tradition meet new ideas and technology. Using silk screen, CNC-milling, letterpress and laser cutting under the same roof, the world of printmaking is presented with a whole series of new opportunities.

[3] Fellesverkstedet – letterpress department, 2014
(overleaf)

-138

[4] Fellesverkstedet – screen-print department, 2014

[5] Christopher Nielsen – 'Rulletrappen', screen print, 2013

FORAN

FELLESVER

TOY MAKIN

BY IRISH DESIGNER GORDO

A BASIC INTRODUCTION TO
ENVIRONMENT, HAND TOO
TOOLS, AND MOST IMPO
CAPABILITES AND BE A

2 NIGHTS OF WORKI
UTTING, FINISHIN
D ASSEMBLIN

SJONSPLASS I 2014
/ ALLE SKALAER

[1] Studio launch invite, letterpress, 2013

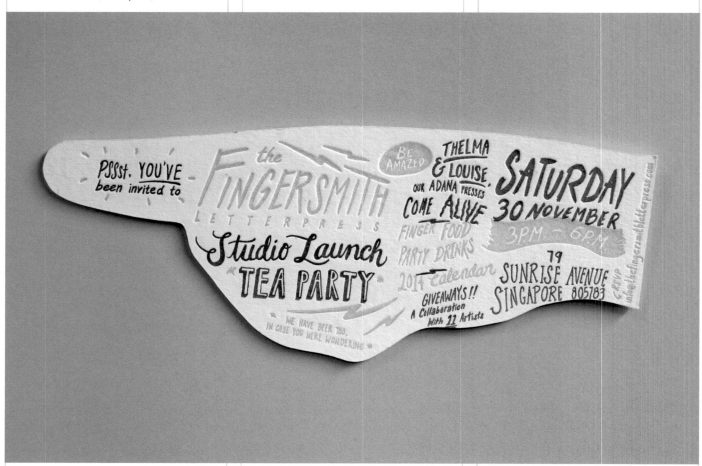

The Fingersmith Letterpress

Letterpress
Singapore

Growing up, Jackie Goh always had an eye for the funny, the weird and the quirky. These whimsical elements soon found their way into her daily life via her illustrations, crafts and film photography. Jackie's relationship with letterpress printing began in an undergraduate lecture about forgotten crafts at LASALLE College of the Arts, Singapore. It was geeky love at first sight. Her curiosity piqued, she took a month-long trip to learn more about the craft through an apprenticeship with a retired printer in Australia. Upon returning, The Fingersmith Letterpress was born.

Operating out of a little shed in her backyard, Jackie began producing small prints such as name cards using 'Thelma and Louise', as she calls her two Adana 8x5 table-top presses. Wanting to expand her production beyond small prints, she searched locally for a bigger press, the Heidelberg. It seemed almost impossible. Just as she was about to give up and put in the order for a Heidelberg from Germany, she got to know of an abandoned Heidelberg through a family friend. She rescued it, restored it to its former glory and named it 'Klaus'.

Letterpress is pretty much an obsolete printing method in Singapore as people tend to look for low-cost printing with a fast turnover. Despite much criticism and scepticism from digital printer operators, Jackie strives to revive this traditional form of printing. However, she injects a contemporary twist in all her designs (mainly with the use of quirky illustration and hand lettering) to appeal to a younger clientele – a fusion of nostalgia and a dash of the loony.

The joy of receiving a unique piece of print that has been artistically crafted is second to none and she

[3] Promotional coasters, letterpress printed, 2013
(overleaf)

Don't drink and drive. If you must, drive someone crazy. A friendly message by...

Don't drink and drive. If you must, drive so...

you can
read this,
you need
another
Bottle!

crazy. A friendly message by The Fingersmith Letterpress.

...gersmith Letterpress.

...and drive. If you must, drive someone crazy. A friendly message by The Fingersmith Letterpress.

A friendly message by The Fingersmith Letterpress.

[5] Singapore postcard series, letterpress, 2014

[6] Logo design and packaging, letterpress, 2014

[7] Christmas postcard series, letterpress, 2013

hopes that the craft can be preserved for generations to come. When not scrubbing the paint off 'Klaus', with gloves, or perfecting her latest works of art, Jackie teaches children to paint. Their wonder and imagination constantly lently inspire her and remind her that the world is what you view it to be – and for Jackie, it still looks very quirky.

[1] Bastonnade, screen print, 2013

[3] Bastonnade, screen print, 2013
(overleaf)

Frenchfourch

Illustration, printmaking
Paris, France

Frenchfourch, established in 2007, is a studio and an independent publishing house based in Paris, France. They manufacture books, posters and T-shirts and organize art exhibitions. Their goal is to highlight the young, flourishing and talented scene of French, European and world graphic artists. Over the course of their projects, they became editors and thus printers – more precisely, screen printers. They define themselves as ink aficionados: they love paper, handmade objects and attention to detail. Screen printing is a semi-artisanal technique whose final product can vary from the textured to the precise. It can intervene in any part of the manufacturing process, it can adapt to everything. It offers an unequalled quality of flattened colours and transcription that can print any kind of image. Every new project for Frenchfourch is a chance to develop their own research and ask new questions. Their most recent screen-printing project, 'Bastonnade', is a road trip in seven countries showing huge screen-printed posters and featuring a new installation with a new collective in each city.

ADRIAN FORROW

[4] Bastonnade Shanghai, screen prints, 2013

Artists:
Antoine Caecke, Hicham Amrani, Daniel Abensour, Vincent Godeau, 910DO, Olivier Koa Cramm, Ludmilla Cerveny, Mathieu Desjardin, Adrian Forrow, Emmanuel Kerner – Naço Gallery, Shanghai

Artists:
Valfret Banzai, Adrian Forrow, Sébastien Touache, Tristan Pernet, Pol Edouard Flores, Tamas Pal, Ludmilla Cerveny, Simon Thompson, Franck Pellegrino, Alexandre Centazzo and Céline Guichard

[5] Happy New Year, screen prints, 2013

[6] Suck, screen print, 2013

[7] Bastonnade Budapest, screen prints, 2013

Artists:
Nicolas Barrome, Antoine Caecke, Clément Vuillier, Diane Boivin, Alex Chiu – Design Terminal, Budapest

[8] Bastonnade ZERO, screen print, 2012

[1] Untitled 14, screen print, 2013

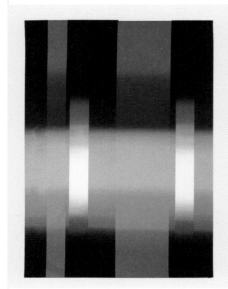

[2] Untitled 12, screen print, 2013

[3] Untitled 15, screen print, 2013

[4] Untitled 11, screen print, 2013

Gfeller + Hellsgård

Illustration
Berlin, Germany

Swedish-French artist duo Anna Hellsgård and Christian 'Meeloo' Gfeller, now based in Berlin, have been working together since 2001, creating and producing prints, artists' books, sculptures, zines and more in their print studio Re:Surgo!, cementing their reputation as master silk screeners and innovators of the medium with every new project. Gfeller's incessant artistic output began in 1995, when he started making punk zines under the name Bongoût. From day one of their collaboration, Hellsgård and Gfeller have placed as strong an emphasis on intuition and skill as on DIY ethics and communal practice, in frequent collaborations with other artists on print projects, organizing exhibitions, and opening their independent artist space and retail store in Berlin to international artists and musicians. They are perfectionists in terms of technique, and their sought-after limited-edition prints are meticulously produced from start to finish.

Throughout the years, their desire to never repeat themselves and to pursue formal innovation and challenging visual content has animated every project and inspired further experiments. In their quest to constantly test and push the boundaries of the medium, they have begun to deconstruct its conventions, techniques and formal structures. Their series of monoprints 'Bad Printing' illustrates this intention to question the familiarity of the silk-screening process, as it consciously highlights – and celebrates – its idiosyncrasies. Across the intentional overlaps, smudges, bleeding, glitches and transparencies we can recognize, in the two

[6] Spread from Trinity Trilogy Triptych, screen print

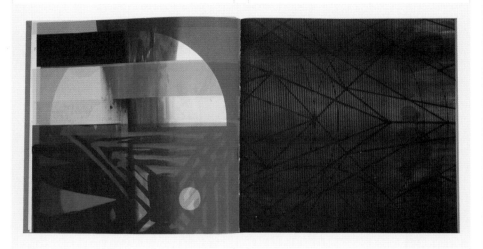

[7] *The Prince*, 1532 (The Father), screen print, 2014

dimensions, a temporal axis as well, a decidedly analogue visual chronology of becoming. As such, each unique print is conceived like an experimental painting, in which accidents and errors play an important part. This resonates with one of their favourites, German painter Georg Baselitz, who described his approach as a struggle, a taming, a negotiation with the image in becoming: 'I begin with an idea, but as I work, the picture takes over. Then there is the struggle between the idea I preconceived . . . and the picture that fights for its own life.' Experimentation can never be

about control. For Hellsgård and Gfeller, it is also, importantly, about un-learning. Chance is given a new prominence in the 'Bad Printing' series. Using investigations into different intensities of abstraction and aleatory geometry, more intuitive than mathematical, these prints create an evocative fractal landscape of shapes, colours and depth. With their series of unique books, such as *The Idiot*, *The Stranger* and *The Prince*, Hellsgård and Gfeller have also rethought the format of the book. Each of the books in this series is titled after a canonic literary work and, with its solemn cover

and precious binding, like an original manuscript, prompts us to rethink the understanding of what a book is, how it is made, how it circulates as a material object and how it mediates its content. Each page is a unique print, and on each the pictorial references and figurative elements disintegrate and realign into an abstract composition across the multiple planes of the image. Echoing its literary namesake, a dense visual narrative emerges across the pages of each book.

[8] *The Stranger*, 1942 (The Son), screen print, 2013

[9] *The Idiot*, 1869 (The Holy Spirit), screen print, 2013

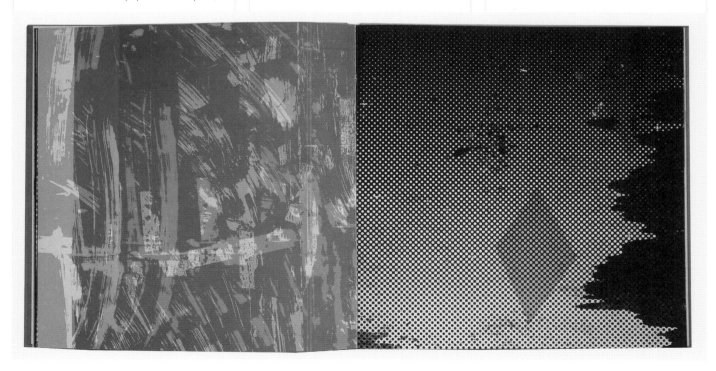

[10] Bad Printing 06, screen print, 2013

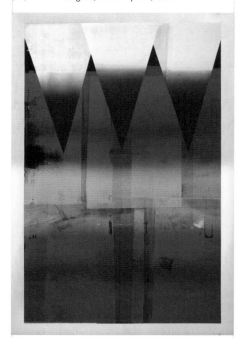

[11] Bad Printing 11, screen print, 2013

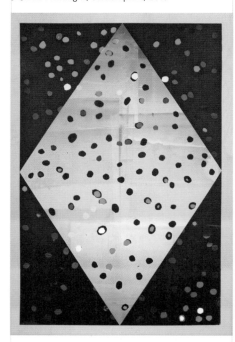

[12] Bad Printing 16, screen print, 2013

[13] Bad Printing 14, screen print, 2013

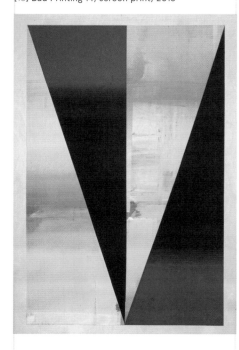

[14] Bad Printing 18, screen print, 2013

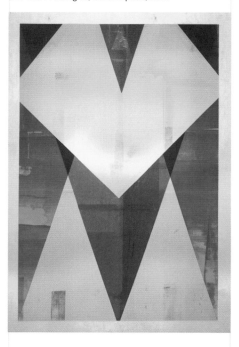

[1] Prove How Easily You Can Have It, letterpress and collage, 2010

GrandArmy

Illustration, printmaking
New York City, New York, USA

The creative team GrandArmy has, among other things, launched an art magazine, branded public schools, written short films, worked in fashion, music and art, shown in gallery exhibitions on both coasts of the United States, painted murals, founded a furniture brand, designed a line of skateboards, and blown up several race cars. GrandArmy is a creative studio in New York City specializing in creative direction and strategy in advertising and graphic design, video concept and direction, branding, custom typography, illustration and printmaking. Some of its earliest works were born on a Vandercook press, exploring the finer points of letter-spacing and composition. As the scope of its work grew to include a spectrum ranging from boutique fashion brands to multinational corporations, the studio has never abandoned its roots in letterpress and analogue processes. GrandArmy continues to experiment on the press every year.

...EL AND I HAD LUNCH IN A LITTLE REST-AURANT NEAR THE PARK.

...CLE NED WILL ...VER APPROVE ...OUR MARRIAGE, ...EL. LET'S ...OPE—TODAY!

BUT, DARLING, WHAT IF YOUR UNCLE CARRIES OUT HIS THREAT AND CUTS OFF YOUR INHERITANCE? I HAVE TO SUPPORT MY SISTER IN TEXAS, AND I'D HATE TO SEE YOU DEPRIVED OF THE THINGS YOU'RE USED TO.

I THINK IT'S DISGRACEFUL THAT YOUR SISTER RAN THROUGH HER OWN MONEY AND NOW IS MAKING A DENT IN YOURS. IF ONLY I COULD MAKE UNCLE NED UNDERSTAND!

YOU WI... HE MA... STUBB... BUT SO... AND YOU... GET YOUR... THE...

[4] Could This Happen Here, letterpress, 2010

[5] Could This Happen Here, letterpress, 2010

[6 & 7] Prove How Easily You Can Have It, letterpress and collage, 2010

[8] Carnival of Values, letterpress, 2009

[1] Jeremy Maxwell Wintrebert, black foil / lasercut / litho, 2013

[2] ArtFad, offset, 2013

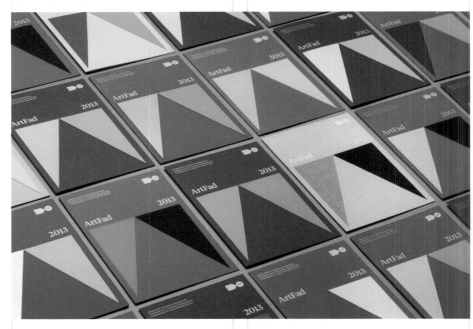

Hey

Graphic design, illustration
Barcelona, Spain

Hey are a design studio based in Barcelona, consisting of Verónica Fuerte, Ricardo Jorge and Mikel Romero. They mostly work in brand identity, illustration and editorial design. They always wanted to have their own style, and they believe they have achieved it. They use geometry, colour and direct typography in a clear, simple manner. When they look back over their work they feel it is consistent; but they usually prefer to look forward.

Their personal projects are almost as important to them as the commercial ones. They let them explore, innovate, push their creative boundaries and meet nice people.

Hey are small. They like it that way because it lets them stay close to their clients, be flexible and take care of every single detail at every step of the process. Among their many clients have been Apple, Monocle, Nokia, the *Wall Street Journal* and Film Commission Chile. In 2013 their exhibition 'Oh my God' at the Mitte Gallery, Barcelona, and Kemistry Gallery, London, presented their original take on the Greek gods in a series of posters.

[4] Léa Munsch Identity, bronze foil, 2014
(overleaf)

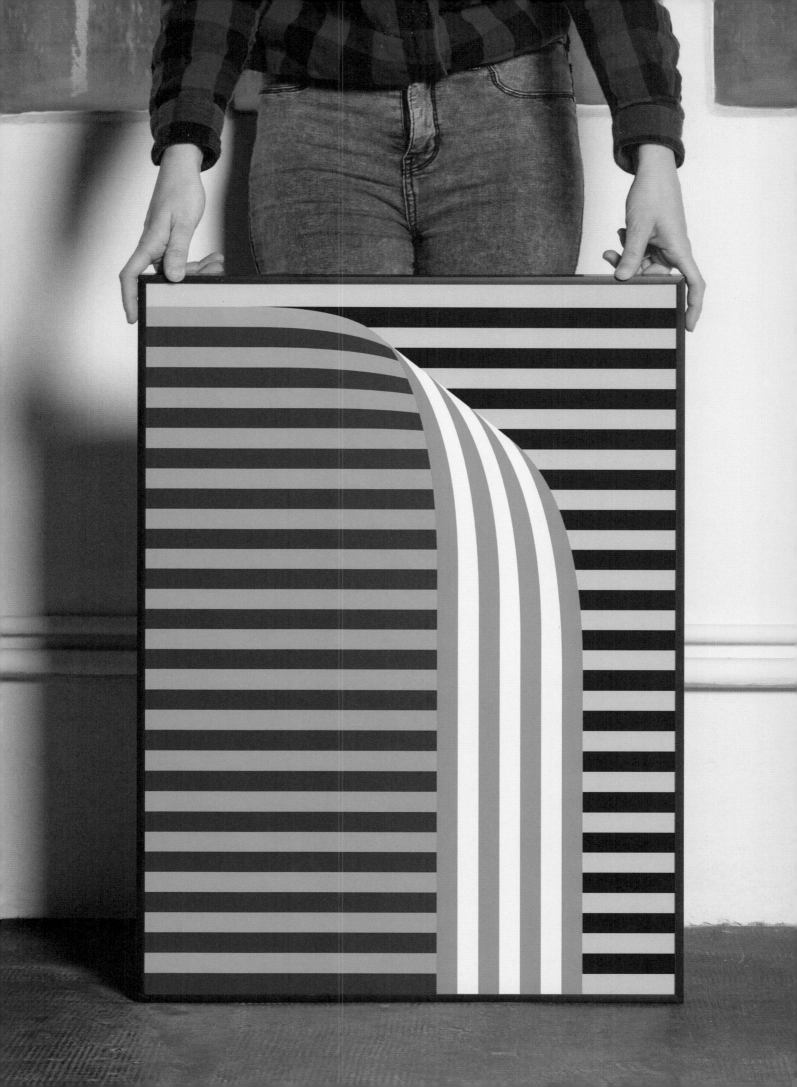

Léa Munsch

leamunsch.com

Creative Management

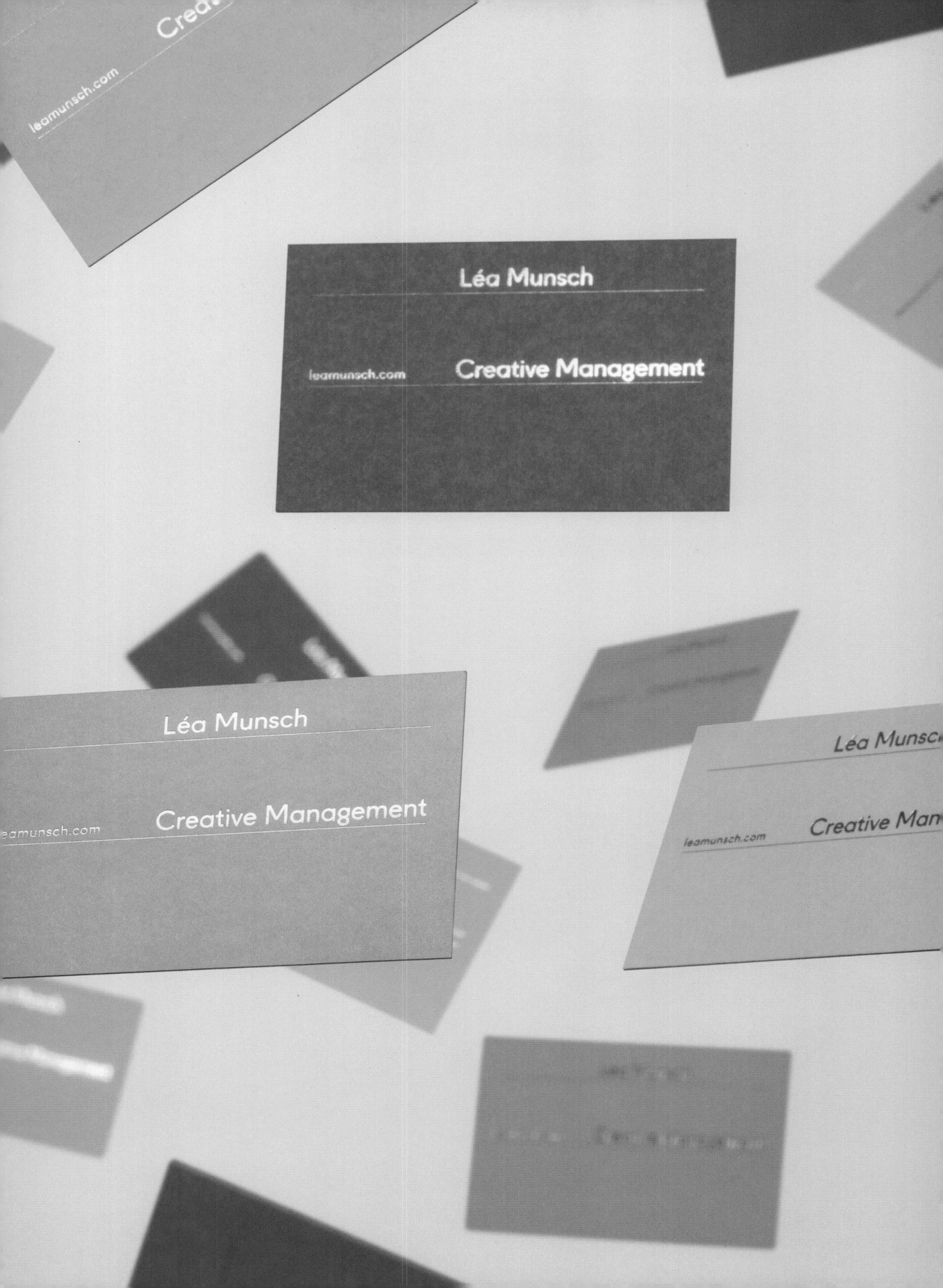
Léa Munsch
leamunsch.com
Creative Management
Léa Munsch
leamunsch.com
Creative Management
Léa Munsch
leamunsch.com
Creative Management

[5] Letter O – Geometric Shadows series, digital, 2014

[6] Agenda CCCB, offset, 2013

[7] Sun, digital, 2014

[8] Sea Stripes, digital, 2014

[9] Gandules'13, offset, 2013

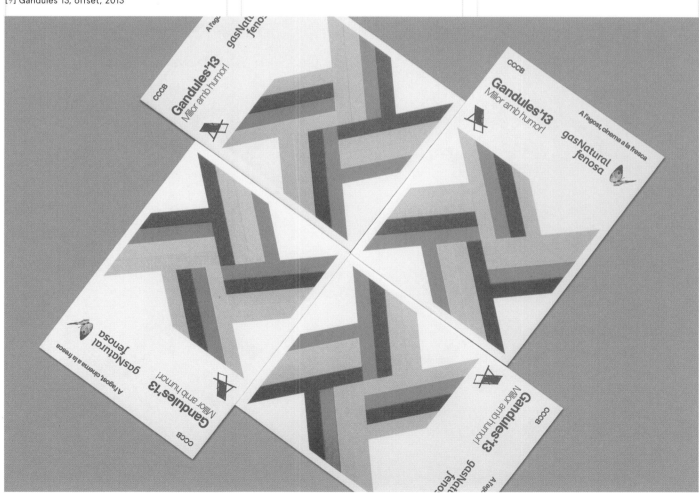

[1] Paper Pyramids for Obus, letterpress / bronze ink, 2013

The Hungry Workshop

Graphic design, illustration
Melbourne, Australia

For the directors, husband-and-wife team Simon and Jenna Hipgrave, The Hungry Workshop is a culmination of their collective interests. They met while studying communication design and some years later began printmaking with letterpress. It made perfect sense to combine the two. Bringing creative services and print production together isn't a particularly new idea. It's a traditional model – one that was born naturally from convenience and necessity at the dawn of printing. It is only in the last hundred years or so that the creative services have been removed from the print production houses. The Hungry Workshop brings back that traditional model, along with all the advances that have been made in design and communication theory. Conceptually driven, articulate design communication paired with functional, tactile and high-quality print production form a perfect counterpoint to the messages we consume daily – commercialized, televised, digitized and compressed for narrow-bandwidth channels. Letterpress production creates the opposite. Letterpress has an enhanced physicality. You can smell, see and touch an idea that has been executed with letterpress. When a design is output in this format it is broadcast in the widest bandwidth we can possibly experience: reality. It is this idea that informs The Hungry Workshop in both design and print work, maximizing the physicality with deep impression and designing with colour so bright your eyes can feel it, creating whatever it takes to snap you out of the digital haze. The Hungry Workshop's workflow reflects their space. It all begins with a tight brief, digitally perfected with accuracy in the studio and then output with press on paper in the workshop.

[3] Aim True, letterpress, 2011
(overleaf)

[4] Aerogram, letterpress, 2012

[5] Aerogram, letterpress, 2012

[6] We Go Together Like Blank and Blank, letterpress, 2013

[1] Tig Bitties, CMYK screen print, 2012

[2] Particles Collide Below The Rising Sea, 2012

Jim O'Raw

Illustration, printmaking
London, UK

Jim O'Raw is a screen printer who lives and works in Hackney, London. He grew up in Birmingham and graduated from Brighton University in 2008. He currently facilitates training courses, experimenting with a wide range of inks and substrates. Having access to such an extensive range of print products has helped develop his personal practice. Exploring CMYK in a variety of tones and opacity is the basis of a lot of Jim's work, creating new compositions through editing and overlaying different layers. Jim has a large collection of books and magazines

from which he draws a lot of inspiration. He states: 'It's the offset lithographic prints some of the older colour images have which I'm attracted to, I especially like when some pages are mis-registered, it's trippy mayn.'

Jim is also one half of the clothing brand BRIDGE UNLTD. Screen printing is important to the garments they create, experimenting with inks and gradients and producing small editions of each design. He has worked closely with People of Print since it started, assisting with workshops, exhibitions and events

across Europe. He intends to carry on exploring print processes inspired by these crucial times, flags and hot sauce.

[5] Mother Universe, CMYK + glow in dark, screen print, 2010

[6] Mother Universe, screen print, 2012

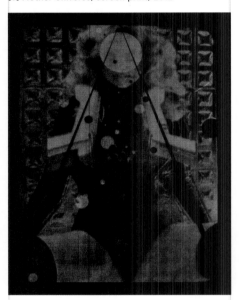

[7] Critical Mass, CMYK screen print, 2012

[8] Iggy, 8-colour screen print, 2014

[1] Pens Are My Friends, digital, 2008

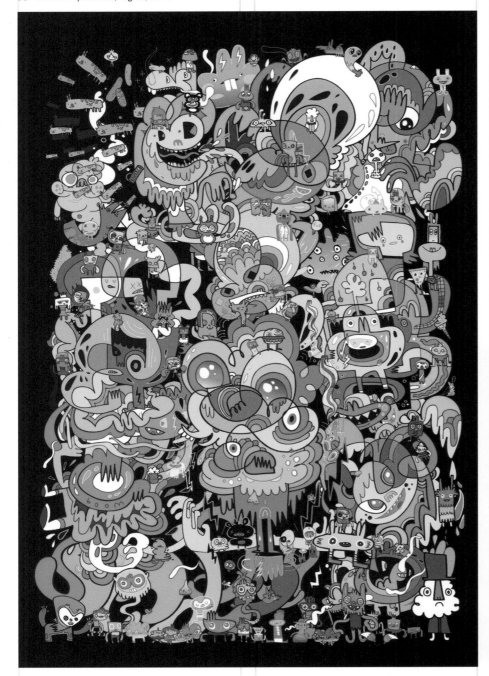

[2] Football, digital, 2012

Jon Burgerman

Illustration, printmaking
London, UK

Jon Burgerman is an award-winning purveyor of doodles. His work oscillates between fine art, urban art and pop culture, using dry humour to reference and question contemporary milieux. His is a pervasive and instantly recognizable aesthetic that exists across a multitude of forms, including canvases, large-scale murals (inside and outside), sculpture, toys, apparel, design, print and people (as tattoos and temporary drawings). His artworks are coveted worldwide and collected in several museums and institutions.

Performance, intervention and active engagement, often direct, with an audience has been prominent within the evolution of his practice alongside his paintings. Burgerman now regularly performs at events, conferences and universities around the world, delivering keynote lectures and running creative workshops. His works include a focus on what he calls 'quiet interventions', where subtle, often cheap, nonpermanent actions drastically (and sometimes comically) alter the reading of a signifier, object or situation. It's

Burgerman's belief that through these playful creative acts, art can act as an agent to change the world, by being the catalyst to allow people to change their own worlds.

[4] Saturday on the Southbank, screen print, 2013

[5] Overground Sooty, giclée, 2009

[6] Burger Family, digital, 2012

[8] Dunno, digital, 2013

[9] Indignation indigestion, giclée, 2012

[10] Alien, digital, 2013

[11] The Love We Feel Is The Love That's Real, giclée, 2011

[1] Kayrock team in studio, 2014

[2] T-Shirt printing press

Kayrock

Printmaking
New York City, New York, USA

Kayrock Screenprinting was started in 1998 by Karl LaRocca (aka Kayrock) in Williamsburg, Brooklyn. After studying printmaking at Oberlin College, Ohio, he began making T-shirts and posters for the local music scene. He soon teamed up with Jef Scharf (aka Wolfy), who brought a hand-drawn style to the collaboration. The pair exhibited at Chelsea gallery Jessica Murray Projects and MoMA PS1 until they ended their collaboration in 2011. Karl moved Kayrock a mile upriver to its current site, a 100-year-old former rope factory in Greenpoint, Brooklyn.

Currently Karl works with a team of six print technicians who share his focus on high-end art editions, producing precise, detail-oriented work. In his own art, mathematics and geometry take the form of an unfolded origami crane, artisanal graph paper or *14 Regular Polygons Approach a Circle*. A passion for running is seen in the NYC Marathon Map and the inspirational *Go Running Every Day* print. Kayrock also publishes printed editions and hand-bound books, regularly exhibiting at the New York Art Book Fair, LA Art Book Fair and EIAB Fair.

Sometimes the worlds of fine art and rock music collide, for example in print editions by Kim Gordon for the White Columns art space. Whether it involves printing tickets for a secret Madonna concert, printing shirts while playing drums with Japanese band the Boredoms, flocking Ray-Ban posters live at a Blondie concert, producing a Marc Swanson edition on giant panels of glass with epoxy ink, or printing a 30-colour paper edition for artistic collaboration FAILE, each day brings different challenges and opportunities to learn and expand their craft.

[5] Wash-out booth

[6] Pulling a print

[7] Pantone book

[1] 115 Years of Heidelberg plaque

[2] Studio

[3] Studio

KeeganMeegan & Co.

Letterpress
Portland, Oregon, USA

KeeganMeegan & Co. of Portland, Oregon, was co-founded by Katy Meegan and Keegan Wenkman in 2007. Primarily known for hand-illustrated relief printing, KeeganMeegan is also recognized for award-winning design and print and packaging solutions for local and global clients, whether for personal, artistic or business needs. Modelled after the job printing shop of yesteryear, it unites illustration and design with printing and die-cutting services, all in-house. KeeganMeegan works with seven Vandercook cylinder presses, primarily used for art editioning services and experimental projects. It also uses two Heidelberg windmills and four Chandler & Price printing presses. KeeganMeegan does job printing that can be coupled with illustration and design. Katy and Keegan's goal is to create hand-crafted, astounding impressions that have both energy and feeling. They love the tradition of letterpress, for its reliability, sustainability, simplicity and tactile feel. Having seen what the best printing can do, in this modern world of immediate gratification and cheap production values, their printing is a throwback to a time when quality and beauty were a necessity in everyday life. They work nationwide with a range of small businesses, design and advertising firms, graphic designers, artists and individuals. By combining their knowledge of design, illustration and letterpress, they work to print beautifully, use the best materials, and support and inspire the local through to the global community.

[5] Katy and Keegan in their studio
(overleaf)

[6] The Joy Formidable, letterpress, 2011

[7] The Men, letterpress, 2012

[8] Cardboard Castle, letterpress, 2012

[9] Rapha business cards, screen print, 2012

[1] Troll Submarine, screen print, 2014

[2] Permanent Summer, screen print, 2013

Killer Acid

Illustration
New York City, New York, USA

Rob Corradetti is an artist living and working in Brooklyn, New York. His work spans a wide spectrum, from intricately lined, neon-infused illustration to lighthearted troll doodles. Often described as trippy or melted, Rob's screen prints are a marriage of detailed pen-and-ink drawings, cut-and-paste collage, and psychedelic pop colours. Beyond a simple synthesis of muck and monsters, they swarm with an otherworldly lyricism, offering a safe haven to rock 'n' roll burnouts, satanic pizza creatures, trollish lurkers and perverted aliens alike.

Rob got his start in printmaking as a teenager, when he wandered into a T-shirt shop in Ocean City, Maryland. His father encouraged him to show his sketchbook to the owner, a musician by the name of Tres Denk. Tres and his parents took a liking to Rob and hired him as the shop apprentice. Throughout the summer, Rob was paid (mostly in T-shirts) to learn the finer points of screen printing. This inspired him to create his first brand, Craggy Sun, a collection sold primarily from the trunk of his car to friends, townies and random hippies in the park.

After graduating from the University of Delaware, Rob migrated to New York with friends, where they began performing music under the name Mixel Pixel. More than a band, they were an audio/video experience, touring extensively during the 2000s. During this time, Rob created numerous posters, zines and T-shirts to sell on the road. These early DIY ventures would subsequently come to inform his work. In 2010, having informally retired from music, Rob started Killer Acid, a print-based art project focusing on screen-printed

[6] Frogs 'n' Flies, screen print, 2011

[5] Troll Variations, screen print, 2011

[7] Mom, screen print, 2012

posters, T-shirts, stickers, pillows and other products. Killer Acid is a self-described celebration of old-school psychedelic poster art, incorporating references to drug culture, American kitsch, surrealism, *Star Wars*, Picasso and Pink Floyd. Some notable Killer Acid products include Troll Variations and Troll Submarine, two black light posters printed in collaboration with Haven Press. Killer Acid also collaborates with Desert Island, a comics, art and novelty shop in Brooklyn. Rob's prints have featured at the International Print Center New York, the Museum of American Illustration, Giant Robot, Printed Matter, and the Print Center in Philadelphia. His work has appeared in *Juxtapoz*, *Vice*, *BUST*, *Smoke Signal*, *WRAP*, *Status* magazine, and *The Washington Post*. Rob has created artwork for bands including Thee Oh Sees, Man Man, Ty Segall, the Black Lips, Mac Demarco, the Pizza Underground, and many more. When he's not printing, Rob can be found playing pinball, drawing in his notebook, or selling T-shirts (to hipsters now, not hippies) from the trunk of his car.

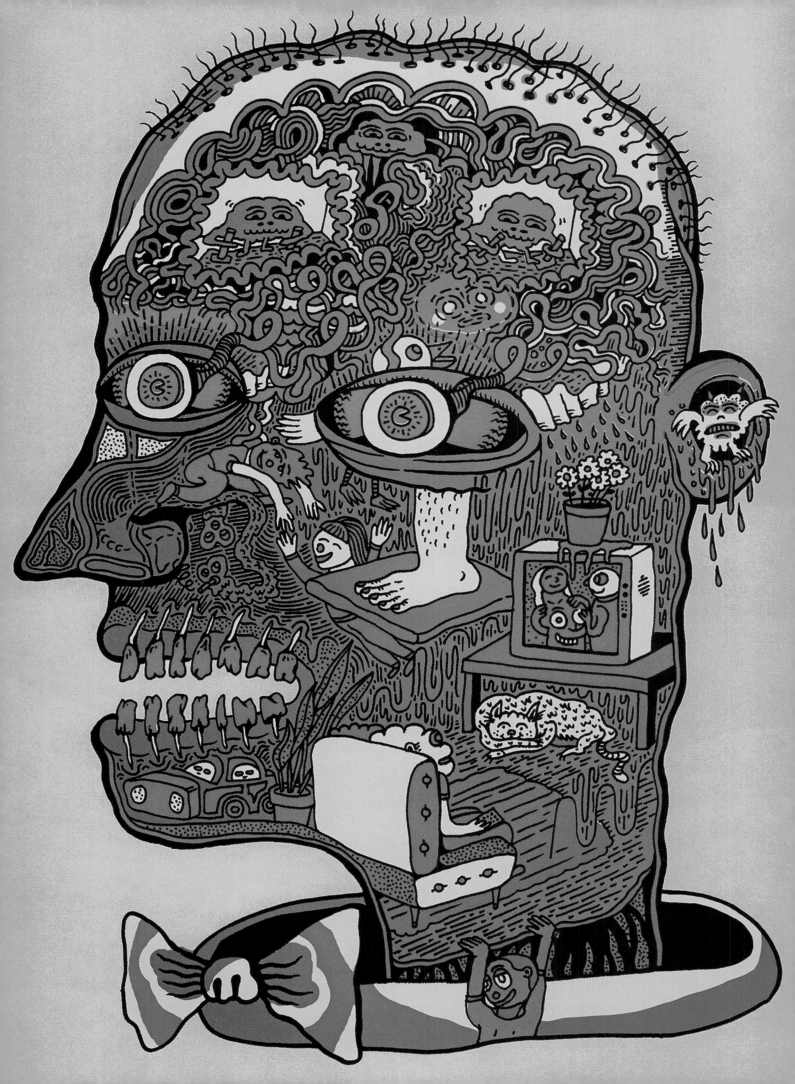

[1] Moiré Sun, screen print, 2013

[2] Studio equipment

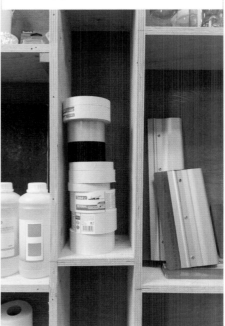

KOPIJ

Printmaking
Hasselt, Belgium

Our globalizing society has had to surrender to the digital culture over the past decades. On a daily basis and in a dazzling tempo images and signals are fired upon us, influencing the way we look at our lives. The digital tools for making and spreading these images are easily accessible and dead simple to use. In several places in the world 'print clubs' have emerged, bringing together a new generation of image makers and graphic designers. They react against the speedy digital design culture by using analogue printing techniques to produce graphic design. KOPIJ is such a print club, serving as an open workspace for graphic experiment and a meeting place for print lovers and analogue loyalists; acting as a forum for debate, knowledge sharing and reflection for graphic artists; and setting up projects dealing with print and its relation to public space. KOPIJ adds an extra dimension to the pure graphical approach: within the social debate it formulates a critical point of view and translates this into graphic design.

[4] KOPIJ print belt, screen print, 2013
(overleaf)

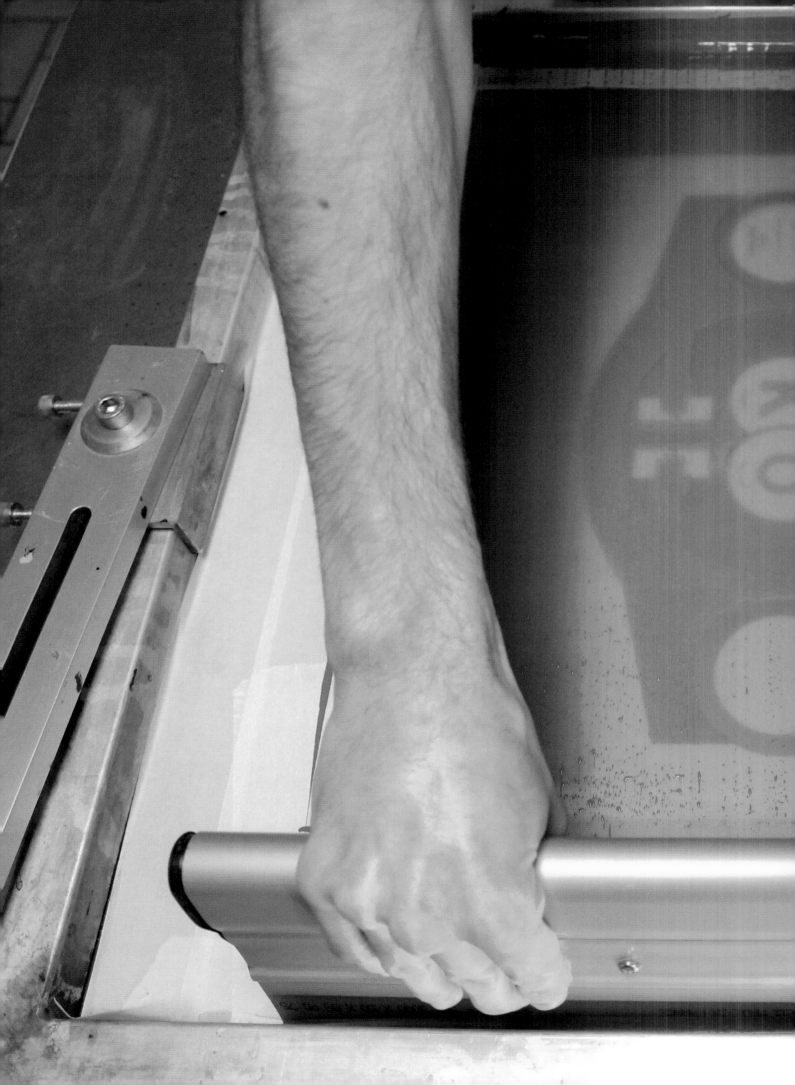

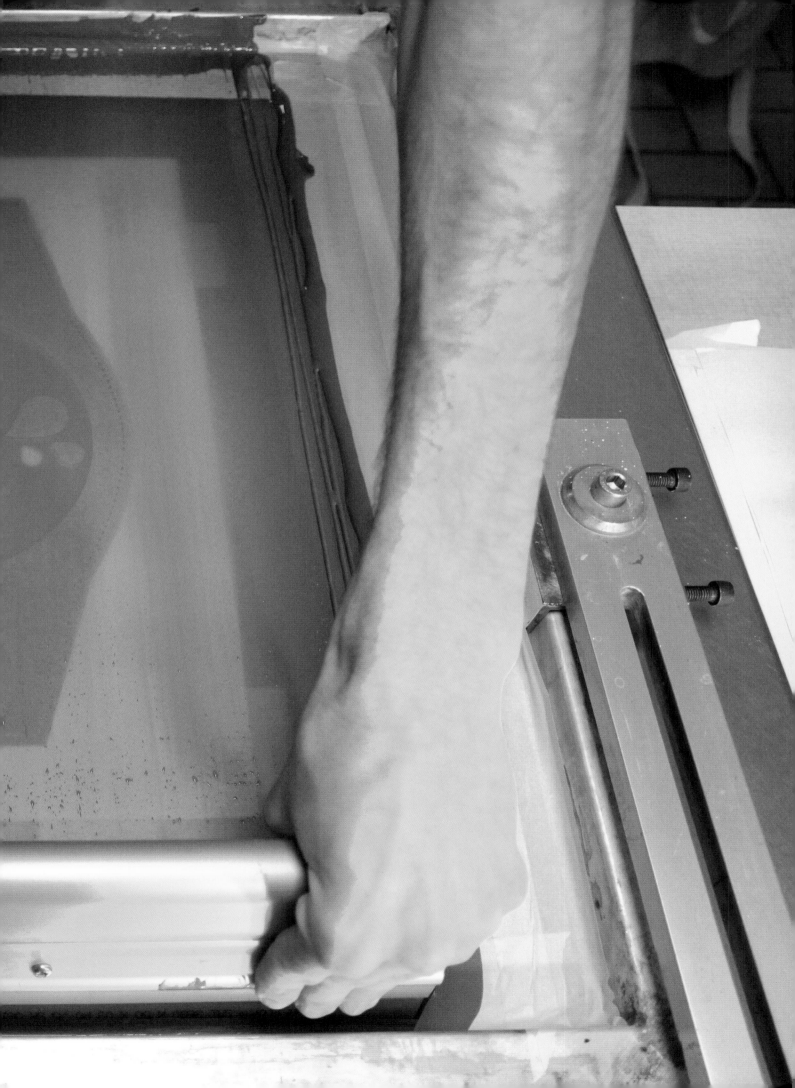

[5] Beginners' silk-screen printing workshop, 2014

[6] KAISER, screen print, 2013

[1] Le Gun Book, Issue 3

[2] Le Gun Book, Issue 5

[3] Le Gun Book, Issue 1

LE GUN

Printmaking
London, UK

Established in 2004, LE GUN is a London-based art collective consisting of five artist-illustrators (Bill Bragg, Chris Bianchi, Neal Fox, Robert Rubbish and Steph von Reiswitz) and two designers (Alex Wright and Matt Appleton), who met as graduates at London's Royal College of Art. As a team of artists they create idiosyncratic imagery, which blends a punk, occult, pop and surrealist aesthetic.

As well as being the producers of their cult self-titled magazine, the group are internationally recognized for their enigmatic installations, design projects and art shows. The particular style they have developed, in which the sum is greater than the parts, is what makes LE GUN's group aesthetic so distinctive. Their independent narrative publication provides a common ground for both emerging and established artists, illustrators, writers and poets.

[6] Bricklayer's Pub, poster and billboard campaign, 2013

[7] Shoreditch High Street, poster and billboard campaign, 2013

[1] Défense de Flâner, screen print, 2014

[2] Surprises 2 Dollars, screen print, 2014

[3] Brussels coasters, screen print, 2011

Les Tontons Racleurs

Printmaking
Brussels, Belgium

Les Tontons Racleurs are a creative duo consisting of Maud Dallemagne and Nicolas Belayew. Based in French-speaking Belgium, they mainly use DIY screen printing as their medium of choice. They met during their degree at ERG (École de Recherche Graphique, Brussels). Both are illustrators, graphic designers, art teachers and screen printers. After graduation, they wanted to keep some time aside from their jobs to keep on creating and printing, so in 2010 they set up their own screen-printing studio, mainly made from second-hand and DIY equipment.

They started to print on a wide variety of supports, from the classic posters and T-shirts to books, wood boards, and more. They alternate between commissoned work (for bands, artists, shops, individuals), self-initiated projects, collaborations and residencies. Most of their projects reflect the time, place or context in which they were made. They often use found objects as a source of creativity, distorting them through their process. They like to experiment with the process in the studio, loving split fountains, overprinting and

cutting papers as positives. Screen printing allows them to play with the richness of colours, with textures and with different supports. It is also a way of having all the different steps of creation in their own hands, from drawing to printing and even bookbinding.

In 2011 they ran an art gallery/workspace over six months in the art centre Recyclart, each month inviting other artists to engage on a new collaborative project. The projects went from big installations to book publishing and even an

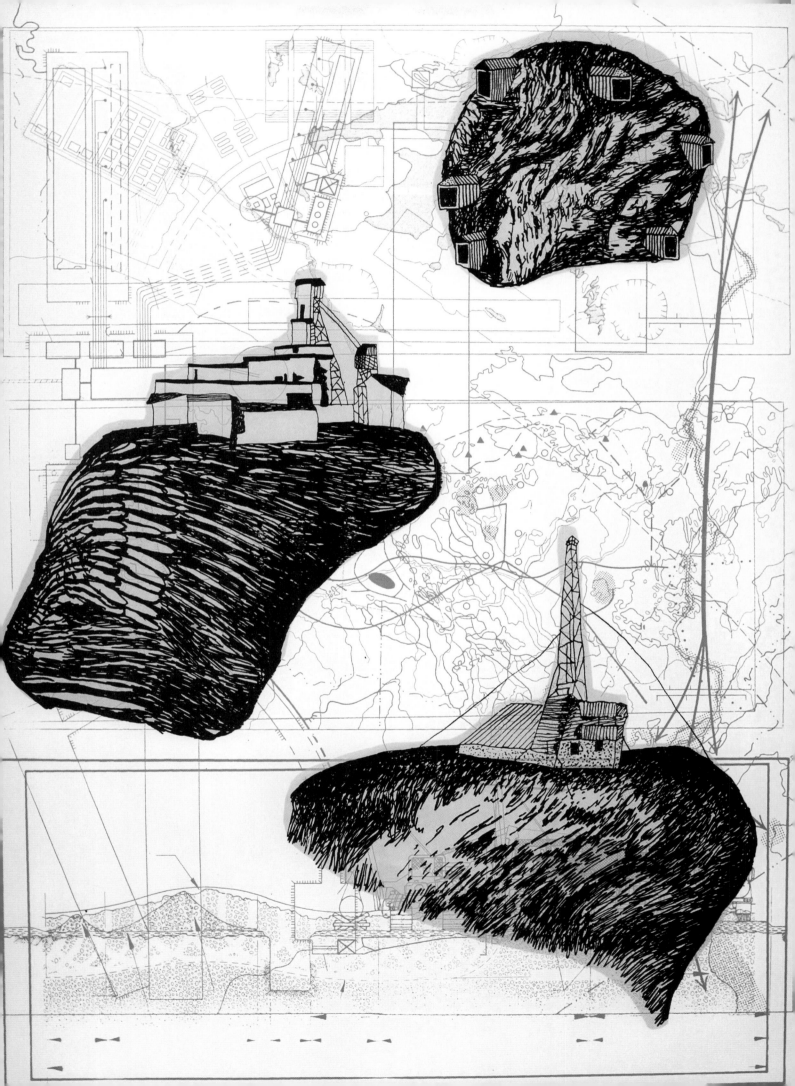

[7—10] Le personnel du ministère de la culture, screen prints, 2014

[8]

[9]

[10]

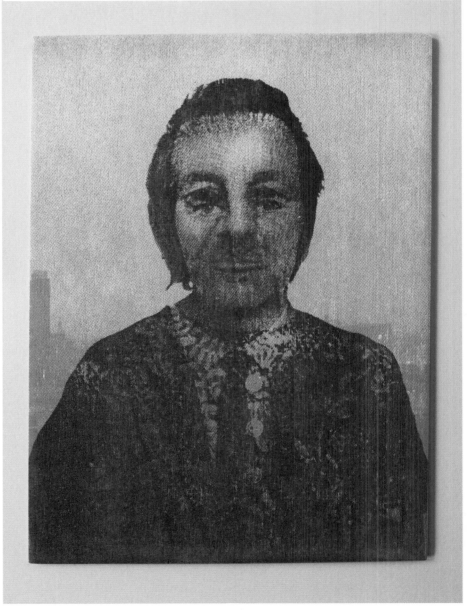

alternative souvenir shop, allowing the visitors to bring home a little piece of Brussels. During the summer of 2012, they were invited for a residency at the Engramme art centre in Quebec, where they spent a month creating new pieces, being inspired by the city and the surroundings, using found material to invent images and create stories around these images. This was also the opportunity to collaborate with local artist OBV.

In 2014 new challenges for the duo included moving their studio from the agitation of Brussels to the quieter and larger spaces of Charleroi, 50 km (30 miles) south of the capital. There they set up a larger and better-equipped studio that would allow them to create more material in a more conducive environment.

LES TONTONS RACLEURS

[1] Unruly And Murderous, pigment print, 2013

Marcus Irwin

Printmaking
Copenhagen, Denmark

Marcus Irwin's graphic collages, serigraphs and digital prints juxtapose popular imagery with chance phrases, combining to expose the incongruousness of context. Print and printmaking have intersected with his work at every juncture, and have been a passion for him since he started reading and collecting comics as a boy, before widening his focus to vintage books, magazines and photographs. Today all forms of analogue and digital printmaking have an influence on his work, and his output covers all forms of production.

Marcus has created print editions and original artworks using techniques as varied as etching, woodblock, screen print, Xerox and pigment printers. He feels that having an understanding of various print processes and their conceptual and historical significance can free him to make aesthetic decisions and judgments that enable him to create work that will resonate with viewers and stand on its own merits once it leaves the studio. 'I once had my work described as a form of anti-graphics. At the time I took it as a kind of

backhanded compliment, but now in hindsight there was something in the work or the way I worked that still resonates now. The work I make can be lo-fi, highly polished, read easily or not immediately understood, but ultimately it is trying to draw the viewer in. It tries to get them to uncover a truth. That may be their truth, my truth or a wider societal truth. It sits there somewhere between the work and the viewer.'

Probably without his realizing it, a large part of Marcus's working environment encompasses

[3] Why?, pigment print, 2013
(overleaf)

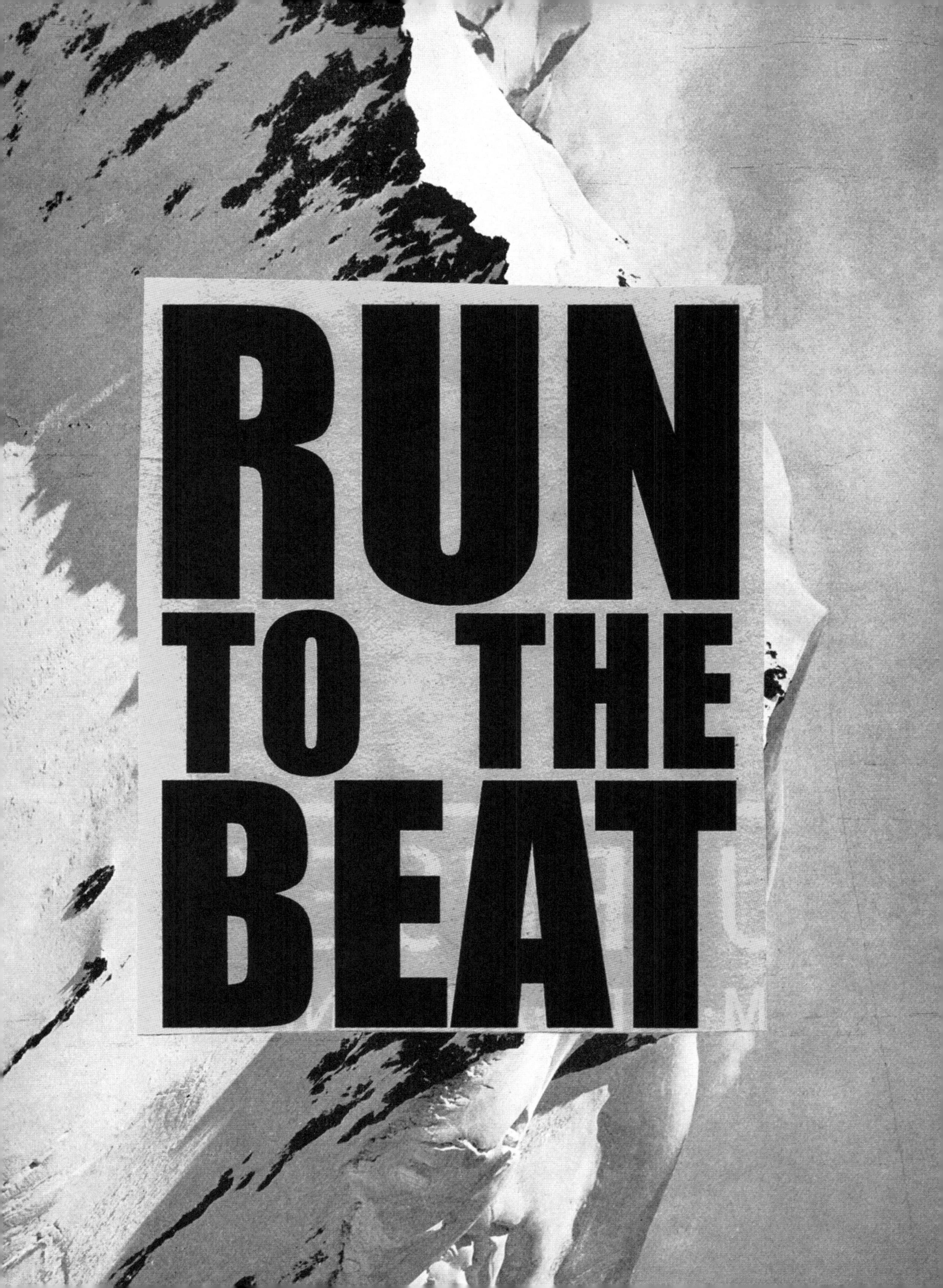
RUN
TO THE
BEAT

WHY
I BE

CAN'T
YOU

[4] Stings, pigment print, 2013

[5] Soft, pigment print / collage, 2014

the time spent outside an actual studio space. The time spent walking between places. Making connections between what is understood outside in the physical tactile environment and attempting to link the nuances of graffiti, the illustrated image and commercial visual language. All of these external influences feed creatively into Marcus's work, and it is here that the interplay between image and text takes shape, along with his desire to explore the rift between so-called high and low culture.

Motifs from movies, television, advertising and the Internet frequently feed into his work. 'It is my aim to use the images that are ubiquitous in our everyday lives to confirm and question the visual language that surrounds us daily. As humans we are endlessly creating images, we create these ideas, we live with them and we can end up believing in them. Print, in whatever form the individual chooses to use it, is really about the dissemination of ideas. I'm interested in the question: "What is the message?"'

[1] PWR RDX 2.0, giclée, 2013

Michael Willis

Graphic art
London, UK

Michael Willis is an English graphic artist based in London, whose work blurs the boundaries between art, fashion, media and image making. His unique visual language with its bright colours and bold lines has gained him notoriety within both the cultural and the commercial sectors. He has worked on transmedia design and direction projects with numerous partners including Kenzo, Bloomberg, It's Nice That, Nike, Urban Outfitters and Mood NYC. In parallel with his freelance practice, Michael is the founder and creative director of the independent online platform worldwide.imgltd.org (formerly known as Panther Club). IMG_LTD is a progressive publishing and collaborative network that aims to promote and support new art, ideas and music worldwide.

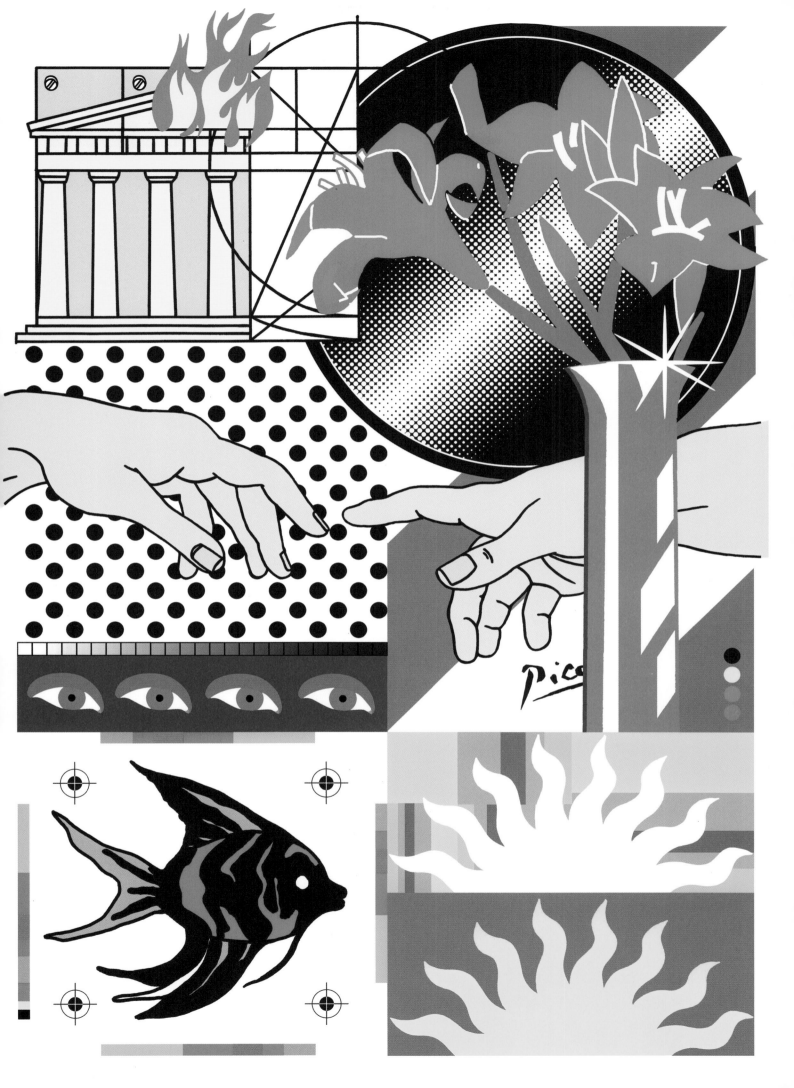

MOONLIGHT

PLEASURE

[5] LIFE, serigraph print, 2013

[6] TIME, serigraph print, 2013

[1] One to the Other, risograph, 2013

[2] Let's Go to the Other Side, risograph, 2013

[3] Natural, risograph, 2013

[4] Flowers and their Homes, risograph, 2013

[5] A Heavy Curtain, risograph, 2013

[6] Doorway, risograph, 2013

Mike Perry

Printmaking
New York City, New York, USA

Brooklyn-based Mike Perry is a designer and artist working in numerous media, including books, magazines, films and newspapers. He draws, paints and illustrates. He animates. He cuts, pastes and builds. He creates sculpture projects and installations. He crafts limited-edition silk-screen posters as well as large-scale advertising campaigns. He curates books and monographs. He can be enlisted to design Mike Perry originals for display at home or office. He gets lost in pattern and wants you to get lost with him, too. He wants to mesmerize

and awaken you through his constellations of line, form, shape, colour, idea. His use of colour, pattern and form expresses a joyful spirit, and while his forms and characters may appear to be childlike, these journeys into our essential existential are not. Perry works regularly for a number of editorial and commercial clients, including Apple, *The New York Times*, *Dwell*, Target, Urban Outfitters, Aldo and Nike. In addition to his commercial, nonprofit and personal artwork, he has also published extensively. His first book, *Hand Job* (2006), paid homage to the

relevance and beauty of hand-drawn type in the digital age. *Over and Over: A Catalog of Hand-Drawn Patterns* (2008) explored the nuanced texture, humour and elegance of illustrative patterns. A third book, entitled *Pulled: A Catalog of Screen Printing* (2011), showcased the silk-screened extravaganza of contemporary artists and designers. His 2012 monograph, *Wondering Around Wandering: Work So Far*, focused on the past eight years of art output.

[8] Giant Zine, screen print, 2010
(overleaf)

THE DUST OF REALITY TRAVELS CONSTANTLY BECOMING A PART OF SOMETHING FOR AS LONG AS IT NEEDS TO. ITS JOURNEY IS ENDLESS AND WITHOUT KNOWING IT WE ARE ALL APART OF THAT DUST AND THAT JOURNEY. A MOMENTARY LOCATION IN A WORLD WHERE TIME IS BEYOND IMAGINATION AND THE TRUE SCALE OF THE UNIVERSE IS KNOWN. DUST IS NOT SOMETHING YOU SWEEP UP. IT IS YOU, ME, MAYBE A CITY, OR THE EARTH. ALL I KNOW IS IT TRAVELS IN AND OUT OF UNIVERSES ON THE BACK OF IMAGINATION FOR ALL OF WHAT IS KNOWN AS TIME. —MIKE PERRY

[9] An Accident Made Good, screen print / ink, 2011
(opposite)

[10] Carrying Modern Art, screen print

CARRYING MODERN ART

[11] Chris's Story No. 2, screen print, 2011

[1] Octopussy, collage, 2012

[2] Suicide Island, collage, 2013

Mojoko

Illustration
Singapore

Born in Iran, raised in Hong Kong, and now based in Singapore, Steve Lawler (aka Mojoko) studied graphic design at Brighton University and undertook a three-year residency at the prestigious Fabrica creative centre in Italy. Jumping between new media, sculpture, screen printing and curating, he is also the owner of a very low-down dirty punk gallery by the name of Kult and runs a quarterly publication of the same name. He has worked and collaborated for more than ten years with some of the world's most exciting artists and pioneers in visual culture. He is currently putting out his own prints and artwork: inspired by being in Asia, his work is a mash-up of east and west. The collision of cultures that he sees around him inspires the maximalist approach taken in the work, which is, in his own words, 'a reaction to the daily bombardment of garbage from television and advertising'.

[5] Play Safe, screen print, 2011

[6] Mojoko Velocet, screen print, 2011

[7] Culture Fuck 1, 2 & 3, screen print, 2012

[8] Tokyo, screen print, 2011

[9] Fantasy Island, screen print, 2011

[10] Big Brother, screen print, 2011

[1] Lost Dunwich, letterpress, 2011

[2] Oranges & Lemons, letterpress / screen print, 2011

New North Press

Letterpress
London, UK

New North Press is an artisan letterpress print studio in London, UK. The press was established in 1986 by Graham Bignell and since 2012 has been a partnership with Richard Ardagh and Beatrice Bless. They have a substantial library of type, which they set and print by hand on Albion presses. Many of their poster editions are inspired by the verbal history of London, from nursery rhymes and folklore traditions to Cockney rhyming slang. They exhibit and sell their work in galleries across the UK. In 2010 they curated 'Reverting to Type', an exhibition of contemporary letterpress artwork, which included the work of twenty presses from around the world. Richard and Beatrice also teach monthly public introductory workshops and produce commissioned artwork such as book covers, film titles and invitations. Clients include Apple, Dulux, HarperCollins, Random House, Penguin and *Wallpaper** magazine. Their book *The Travelling Barmaid* was highly commended in the British Book Design & Production Awards 2009 and shortlisted for the D&AD annual 2008. *Of green leaf, bird and flower*, an artist's book for Mandy Bonnell, is part of the Yale Center of Book Arts collection.

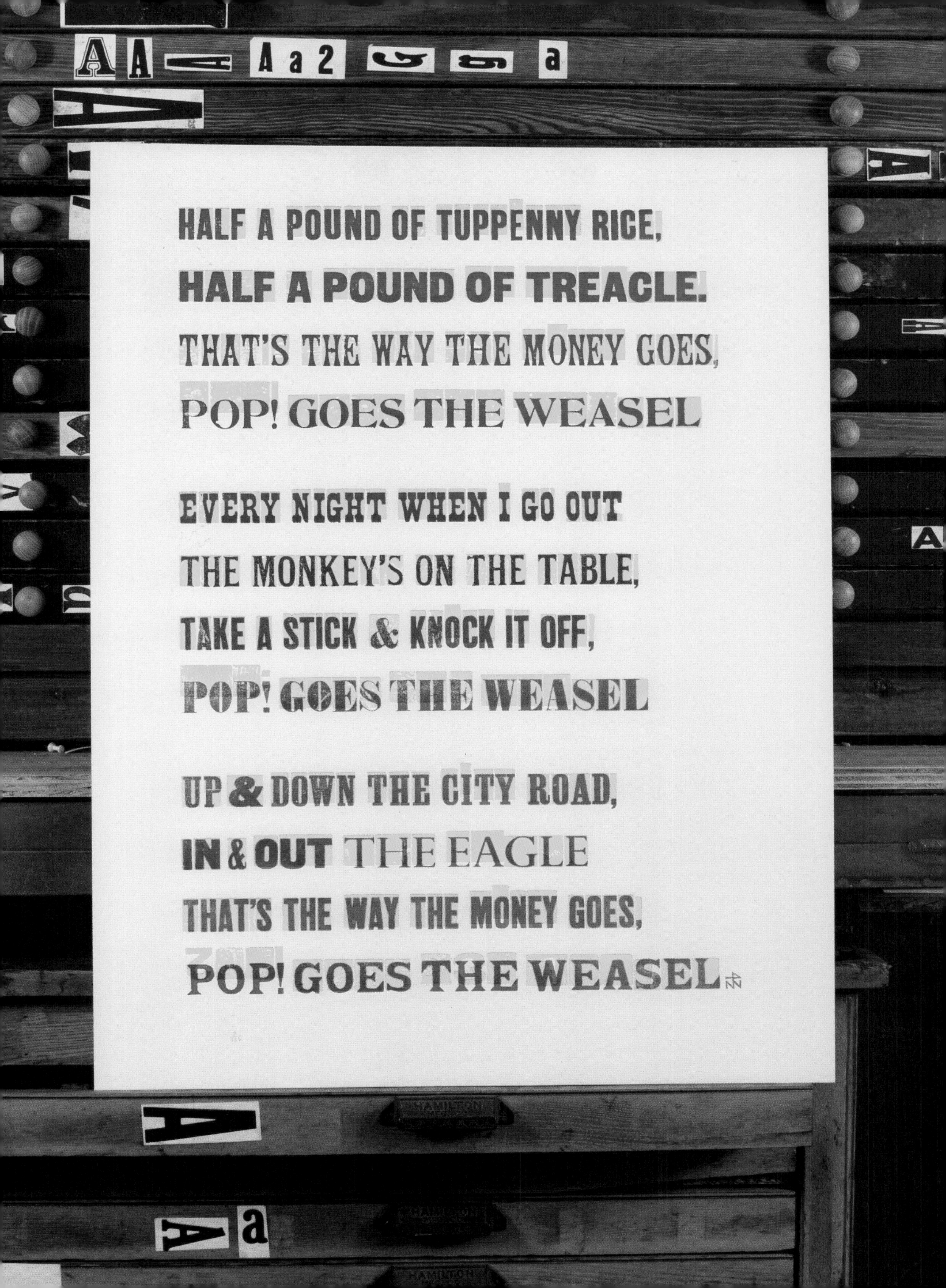

HALF A POUND OF TUPPENNY RICE,
HALF A POUND OF TREACLE.
THAT'S THE WAY THE MONEY GOES,
POP! GOES THE WEASEL

EVERY NIGHT WHEN I GO OUT
THE MONKEY'S ON THE TABLE,
TAKE A STICK & KNOCK IT OFF,
POP! GOES THE WEASEL

UP & DOWN THE CITY ROAD,
IN & OUT THE EAGLE
THAT'S THE WAY THE MONEY GOES,
POP! GOES THE WEASEL

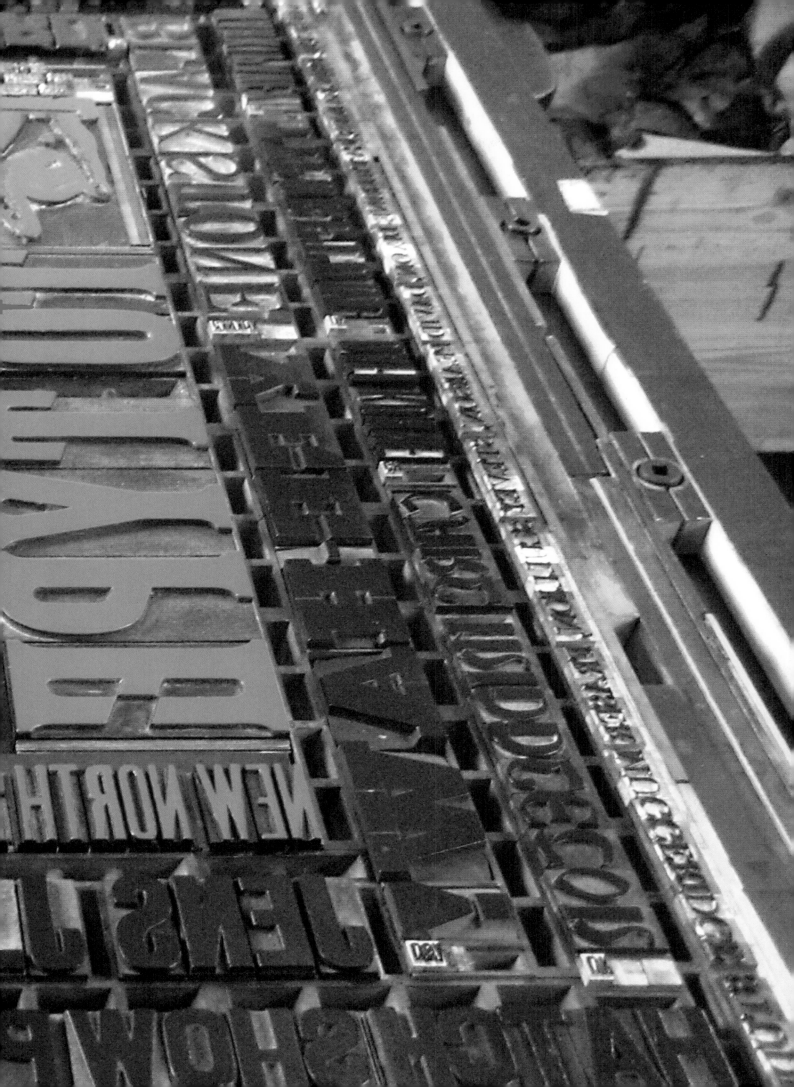

[5] Reverting to Type, letterpress, 2009

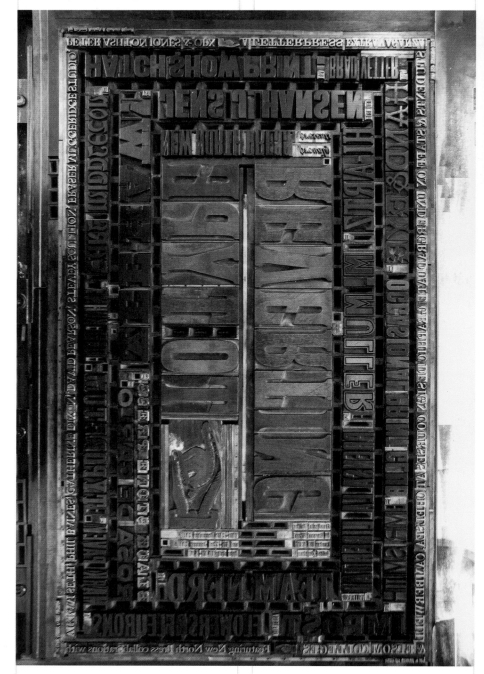

[5] Reverting to Type, letterpress, 2009

[6] London, letterpress, 2013

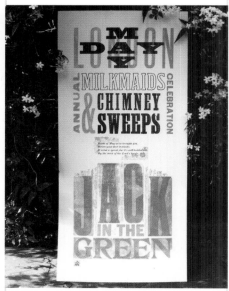

[7] One for Sorrow, letterpress, 2010

REVERTING TO TYPE

NEW NORTH PRESS proudly presents

YEE-HAW!

A LETTERPRESS EXTRAVAGANZA!

by Richard Ardagh & Graham Bignell

Two thousand and ten

PETER ASHTON JONES & OPX

HATCH SHOW PRINT USA

BRAD VETTER USA

JENS J. HANSEN DENMARK

STUDENTS & STAFF ON UNDERGRADUATE GRAPHIC DESIGN COURSES AT CHELSEA, CAMBERWELL & EPSOM COLLEGES

HAND&EYE UK

HI-ARTZ UK

M. MÜLLER CH

OCCASIONAL PRINT CLUB UK

PRENSA LA LIBERTAD ARGENTINA

MR. SMITH UK

CARL MIDDLETON UK

DAFI KUHNE CH

BLACK STONE PRESS CAN

ROSA DE CARLO UK

TYPORETUM UK

MARK PAVEY UK

TEAM NERD USA

IMPOST AUSTRALIA

FLOWERS&FLEURONS UK

Standpoint Gallery
45 Coronet Street
London N1 6HD
United Kingdom

10th-24th December 2010
and 4th-22nd January 2011
Open daily 10 AM - 6 PM

Featuring New North Press collaborations with

VIKRAM SETH, PHIL BAINES, CATHERINE DIXON, DAVID PEARSON, STEVEY SCULLION, FRASER MUGGERIDGE STUDIO

Set & printed by hand

at New North Press, London

[1] PCP studio space, Los Angeles

[2] Tools of the Trade, giclée, 2014

[3] Squeegee wall

Poster Child Prints

Printmaking
Los Angeles, California, USA

Based in Los Angeles, California, Poster Child Prints (PCP) was founded by Sonja Teri to allow collectors to own pieces that might otherwise be inaccessible. 'I think people are intimidated when it comes to buying artwork – the idea can be extremely overwhelming. We hope that by making artwork available at attainable prices, it gives customers a venue to feel safe purchasing artwork they love,' says Teri. Whether a collector is a novice enthusiast or an established connoisseur, PCP sells high-quality prints at modest prices so that art is within the reach of all. Working with a stable of artists from various genres including contemporary art, modern art, and pop art, as well as photography, music, street art and graffiti, PCP consistently delivers the finest prints from a wealth of accomplished artists and rising talent.

Having collaborated with such celebrated artists as Curtis Kulig, Cyrcle, Dabs Myla, Don Pendleton, FriendsWithYou, Neckface, Shepard Fairey and Tim Armstrong, PCP has carved out a unique place in the art world. Along with an expansive list of well-known names, PCP takes great care to spotlight many new and emerging talents, neighbourhood locals and unsung innovators. Teri says, 'One of the main goals with this company is to educate people on why these artists are important and why the quality and craftsmanship of these prints are important.'

With an emphasis on diversity and quality, every PCP edition captures a moment in history. Each print is indicative of a particular stage of an artist's career. PCP does not do reprints. Each print is individually numbered and embossed with PCP's seal. Every

[5] Numbered and embossed, 2014

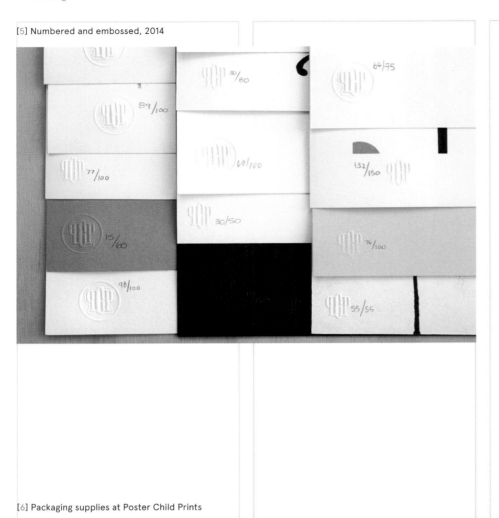

[6] Packaging supplies at Poster Child Prints

[7] Certificate of authenticity, 2014

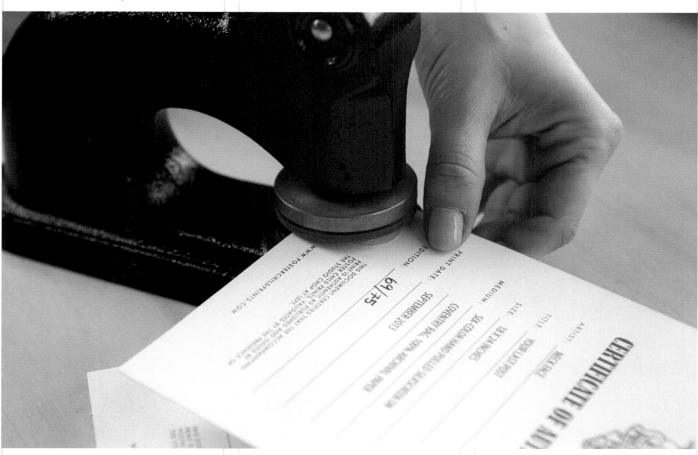

[8] Packaging materials, 2014

[9] 'Obey Peace' series by Shepard Fairey, screen print, 2010

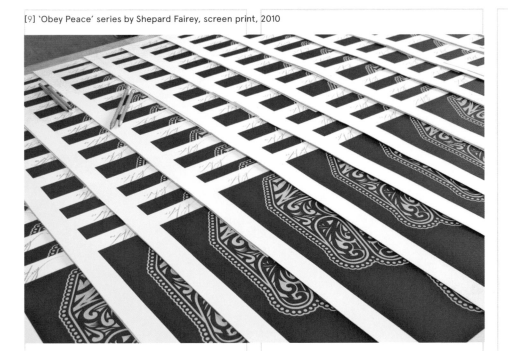

[10] Joshua Petker signing 'Spaghetti Western II' (Artist Edition), hand-painted, 2013

piece is instantly collectable. Teri elaborates: 'Every print comes with a certificate of authenticity; every print has special packaging. I believe presentation is everything, and that's obvious when you receive a package from us.' Based on the world-class stature of its roster of artists and the sterling reputation of PCP as a curatorial force, print editions sell through almost immediately. Ensuring the utmost premium quality for every piece produced is the top priority of PCP. All of their prints are crafted in the United States by master screen printers with decades of experience in the industry. Using only the finest 100% cotton archival papers and industry-leading UV inks that are specifically formulated to withstand the potentially negative effects of time and sunlight exposure, Poster Child prints are created to last.

PCP is on a mission to connect artists and supporters. The prints bridge a gap between worlds. By producing affordable, attainable prints of the highest quality, PCP consistently smashes barriers that are too often imagined to be impossibly exclusive.

[11] PCP studio, 2014

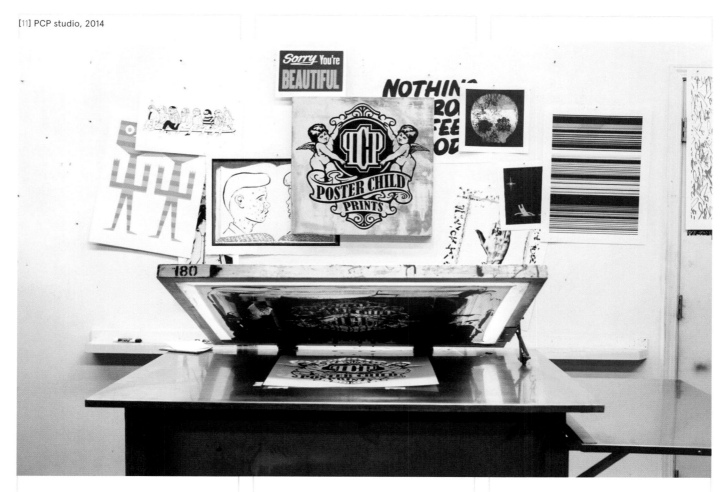

[12] PCP studio space, Los Angeles, 2014

[1] Printing

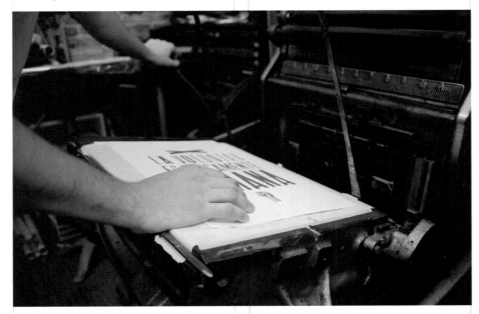

[2] Machinery

Prensa La Libertad

Letterpress
Buenos Aires, Argentina

Founded in 2009, Prensa La Libertad is based in Buenos Aires and strives to rescue forgotten technologies of movable type alongside propagating messages that spring from the daily experiences of city life. The press is run by twenty-eight-year-old Federico Cimatti, a former graphic design student at the University of Buenos Aires, who currently teaches at the same university. He enjoys writing poetry while travelling by bus around the city, and works as a typesetter and printer at his company. Since founding Prensa La Libertad, Federico has met colleagues and printers who share the same passion, allowing him to participate in two joint exhibitions and one individual show. 'Reverting to Type' (December 2010/January 2011) was organized by the New North Press of London and took place at the Standpoint Gallery, London, with twenty participating printers from all around the world. 'Rezo Versos' (2010), organized by Prensa La Libertad, was held at the Hamilton Wood Type & Printing Museum, Wisconsin, and Libros La Teatral, Buenos Aires: this exhibition collected together a selection of posters and pieces that were the result of two years' work. 'Type Impressions' (2011), organized by the Danish printer Jens Jørgen Hansen, took place at the Danish Museum of Media in Odense, and included twenty international letterpress printers.

*TODO LO QUE PASA EN TU CABEZA PUEDE SER REAL

[6] Evangelina Cipriani / Pantalla Cascada, letterpress, 2014

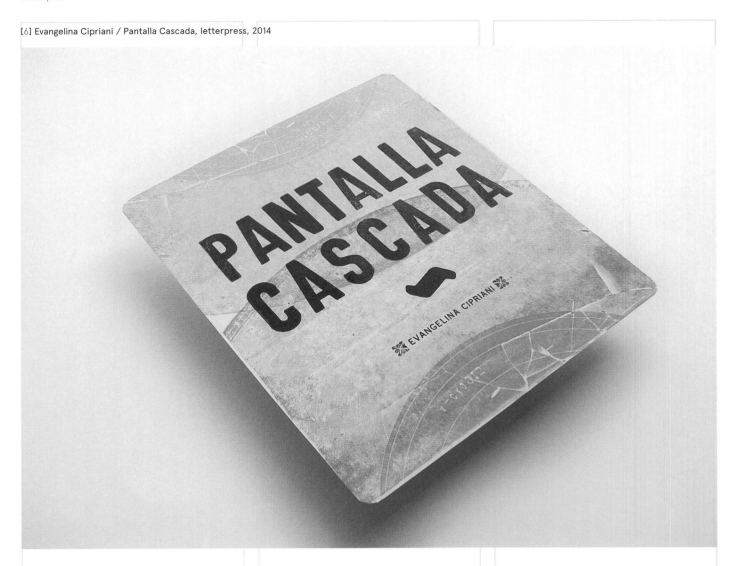

[7] Atención Despierte, letterpress, 2014

[8] Las Cosas, letterpress, 2014

NO QUIERAS NADA PARA TI QUE NO SEA PARA TODOS

TEXTO **ALEJANDRO JODOROWSKY** & FORMA **PRENSA LA LIBERTAD**

[2] Green Hedge, screen print, 2013

[1] Pink Floral Trellis, screen print, 2013

Print Club Boston

Printmaking
Boston, Massachusetts, USA

Created by artist Elizabeth Corkery, Print Club Boston is an online source for limited-edition silk-screen prints. Released as a series in small editions, each collection of prints has a thematic cohesion and production. Originally trained as a printmaker, in much of her work Corkery connects conceptual concerns of repetition, reproduction and simulation with spatial investigations that initiate a slippage between the conventionally two-dimensional nature of print media and a more volumetric architectural space.

Corkery's mode of production often relies on panelling and reproducible modular elements that hinge between mass-produced component parts and bespoke printed forms. Shapes and line repeat and dissolve across separate segmented surfaces resulting in a rhythmic interplay that forces us to reconsider the architectural environment as merely a static backdrop.

Print Club Boston was born out of Corkery's desire to reassert a place for screen print in her daily art practice. As her personal work expanded

in scale to involve larger prints and environmental room installations, she looked to ways she could translate some of her conceptual concerns to smaller, less production-heavy prints that would then be made available online. The themes behind each collection play out in visually diverse ways across the series of prints. The first collection, 'The Grid, The Trellis', takes as its focus the structural geometry of the garden trellis. This form is a commonly used armature for the upward growth of plants, and it simultaneously addresses the

[4] Elizabeth Corkery at work in the studio
(overleaf)

[5] 'Nowhere Is There a Garden', installation, 2013

[6] 'Nowhere Is There a Garden', installation, 2013

potential for fertile expansion and free-form plant life and the unnatural geometric structure of the grid. Corkery examined similar formal structures in her exhibition 'Nowhere Is There a Garden', an installation that explored various historical modes of garden representation and included free-standing green lattice cubes that divided the space and acted as signifiers for the otherwise absent plant life in the gallery. Corkery's ambition for 'The Grid, The Trellis' was to see how a tension could be generated between potential pictorial depth and the imposition of the grid – an ever-present reminder of the inherent flatness of the printed page. Much of the imagery in the prints is sourced from photographic reproductions of formal European gardens. The use of the trellis in formal gardens as a tool for manipulating or ornamentalizing the otherwise natural growth of plants could situate the trellis as a point where art and nature meet the grid.

[1] Sorry I'm Late tank, 2014

[2] DIY Print Shop, screen-print kit packaging, 2014

Print Liberation

Printmaking

Philadelphia, Pennsylvania, USA

Print Liberation started in the late 1990s as two friends – Jamie Dillon and Nick Paparone – printing T-shirts after hours at a local print shop in Dayton, Ohio. It was 1998, the golden age of hip hop was coming to a close, and the first iMacs had just hit the shelves. They borrowed copies of Adobe Illustrator and Photoshop from their high-school vocational programme, uploaded them to the Bondi Blue beast (the original iMac), and the fun began. After some college and a stint in Cincinnati, they moved into a warehouse in Philadelphia with some friends to

live the dream. Time spent working at ad agencies and the opportunity to author a book about how to screen print pushed them to strike out on their own, with a dream to make things for the world and its people on their own terms.

Today, Print Liberation is a full-service creative service agency that works primarily at the intersection of art, design, community and commerce. Jamie and Nick's love for screen printing endures, as they hand-print products (100% made in the USA) in the same Philadelphia warehouse that

welcomed them more than ten years ago. They have worked with everyone from sneaker and alcohol companies to museums and fashion brands to retail spaces and major magazines. Print Liberation T-shirts inhabit every continent on planet Earth, including Antarctica, and have been worn by the likes of Chloë Sevigny and Kanye West. An office in New York and joint ventures such as the DIY Print Shop have helped Print Liberation grow its vision and spread the power of print around the world.

[4] Japanther Poster, black ink screen print, drying rack, 2005
(overleaf)

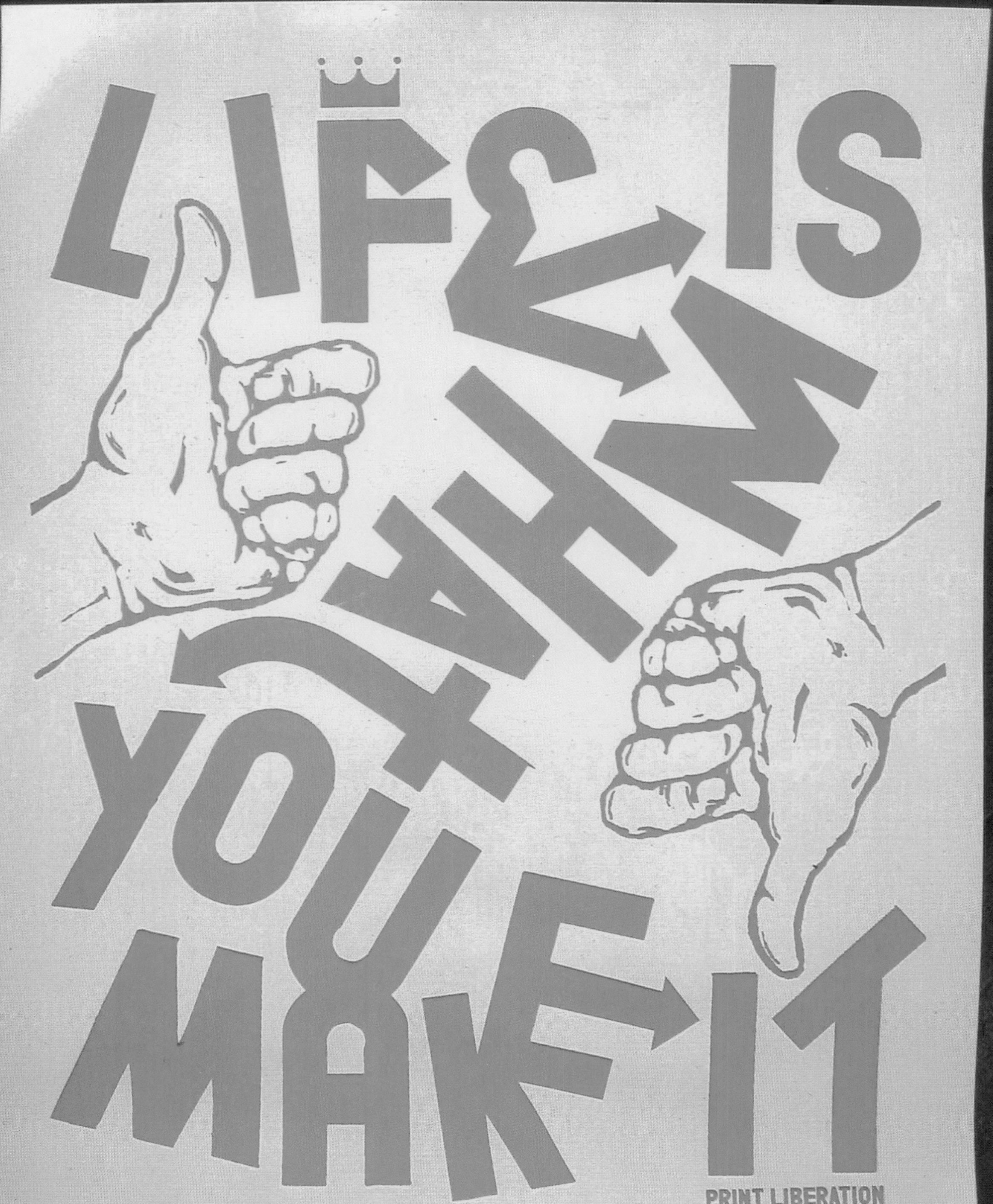

LIFE IS WHAT YOU MAKE IT

PRINT LIBERATION

[5] Pile of screens

[6] Studio wall

[7] Studio bookshelf

SMALL
CHANGE
PRESENTS

A

FAMILY
FINDS
ENTERT-
AINMENT

BY RYAN TRECARTIN

&

PLUS
FILMS BY:
ANDY SPORE
DENA DECOLA
JEREMY BAILEY &
KARIN E. WANDNER

LIVE
PERFORMANCE BY
THE BUNNY
BRAINS

SAT 8:30
JUNE 10 AT
VOX POPULI $6
1315 CHERRY ST
4TH FLR
SMALL
CHANGE
SCREENINGS
.COM

[1] Tagger Scum, screen print, 2010

[2] Why Am I Me And Not You, letterpress, 2011

WHY AM I ME AND NOT YOU

Pure Evil

Street art, screen printing
London, UK

To understand a bit about Pure Evil (real name: Charles Uzzell-Edwards), it is illuminating to know that he is a descendant of Sir Thomas More, the English statesman who wrote the controversial work *Utopia* (1516) and who was later beheaded by King Henry VIII. With this background (Sir Thomas was later canonized) it is perhaps only natural that Pure Evil should explore the darker side of the wreckage of utopian dreams and the myth of the Apocalypse, a belief in the life-changing event that brings history with all its conflicts to an end.

In 1990 Pure Evil left the ruins of Thatcher's Britain for a new life in California, where he became a designer for influential streetwear clothing label Anarchic Adjustment, producing clothes and screen printing T-shirt graphics. He also became involved in the electronic music scene in San Francisco, eventually ending up a recording artist for ambient record label FAX. After ten years in California, influenced heavily by West Coast graffiti artists such as Twist and Reminisce, he returned to London, picked up a spray can and started painting weird

[4] Richard Burton's Nightmare, spray paint and stencil on canvas, 2013

[5] Double-exposure screen print, 5 layers, 2013

[7] Prince Philip's Nightmare,
4-colour screen print, 2013

[6] J.F.K.'s Nightmare, 2-colour screen print, 2012

[4] Richard Burton's Nightmare, spray paint and stencil on canvas, 2013

[5] Double-exposure screen print, 5 layers, 2013

IS WHAT I SEE
AND HEAR AND
SMELL NOT JUST
AN ILLUSION
OF THE WORLD
BEFORE THE WORLD

[10] Darth Typewriter, 3-colour screen print, 2012

[9] Man's Ruin, 2-colour screen print, 2011

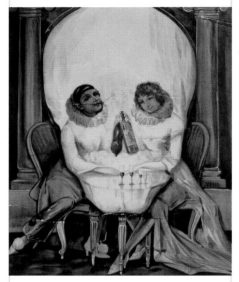

fanged Pure Evil bunny rabbits everywhere. Pure Evil fell in with the people behind Banksy's Santa's Ghetto and started producing prints for Pictures on Walls. He was refused entry back into the USA, and subsequently started plotting and producing dark new prints and artwork in a tiny shed in the Black Mountains of Wales.

After moving back to London, he debuted his first Pure Evil solo show and from the success of that, opened up the Pure Evil Gallery in a Dickensian old shop and basement in Shoreditch in the East End of London in 2007. As an artist, over the past five years Pure Evil has exhibited in China, Russia, Mongolia, Brazil, the USA and all over Europe, and as an 'accidental gallerist' he has produced more than fifty different exhibitions with emerging and established artists at the gallery and internationally. He produces a monthly radio show and regularly gives workshops and participates in lectures about street art.

[1] Darwin Chair

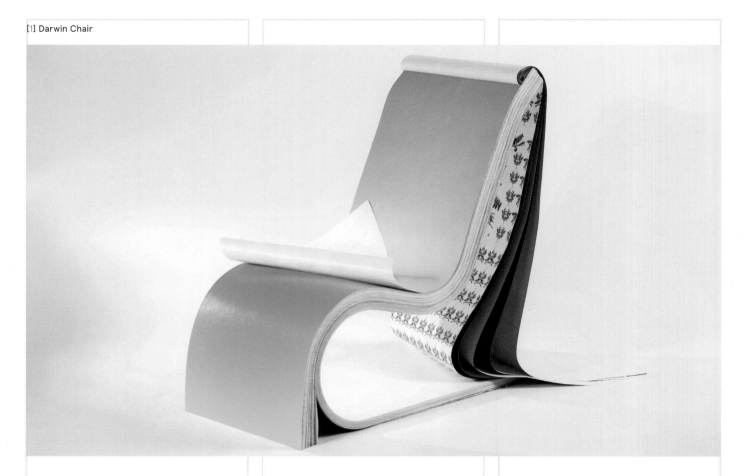

Sagmeister & Walsh

Graphic design
New York City, New York, USA

Sagmeister & Walsh, formerly Sagmeister Inc., is a New York City-based design firm that creates identities, commercials, films, books and objects for clients, audiences and themselves.

Austrian-born Stefan Sagmeister studied graphic design at the University of Applied Arts Vienna. He later received a Fulbright scholarship to study at the Pratt Institute in New York. In 1991, he moved to Hong Kong to work with Leo Burnett's Hong Kong Design Group. In 1993, he returned to New York to work with Tibor Kalman's M&Co

design company. That same year he founded Sagmeister Inc. and the company has since designed branding, graphics and packaging for clients as diverse as the Rolling Stones, HBO, the Guggenheim Museum and Time Warner.

In 2012 Jessica Walsh was added as a partner and the studio was renamed Sagmeister & Walsh. A designer, illustrator and art director, Walsh graduated from Rhode Island School of Design and interned with Pentagram before going to work as an art director for *Print Magazine*. Her work has won

many awards, including from the Type Director's Club, Art Director's Club, *Print* and *Graphis*. She has received various distinctions including *Computer Art*'s 'Top Rising Star in Design' and *Print Magazine*'s 'New Visual Artist'.

Solo shows on Sagmeister Inc.'s work have been mounted in Zurich, Vienna, New York, Berlin, Japan, Osaka, Prague, Cologne and Seoul. Sagmeister's motto, reflected in his studio's work, is: 'Design that needed guts from the creator and still carries the ghost of these guts in the final execution.'

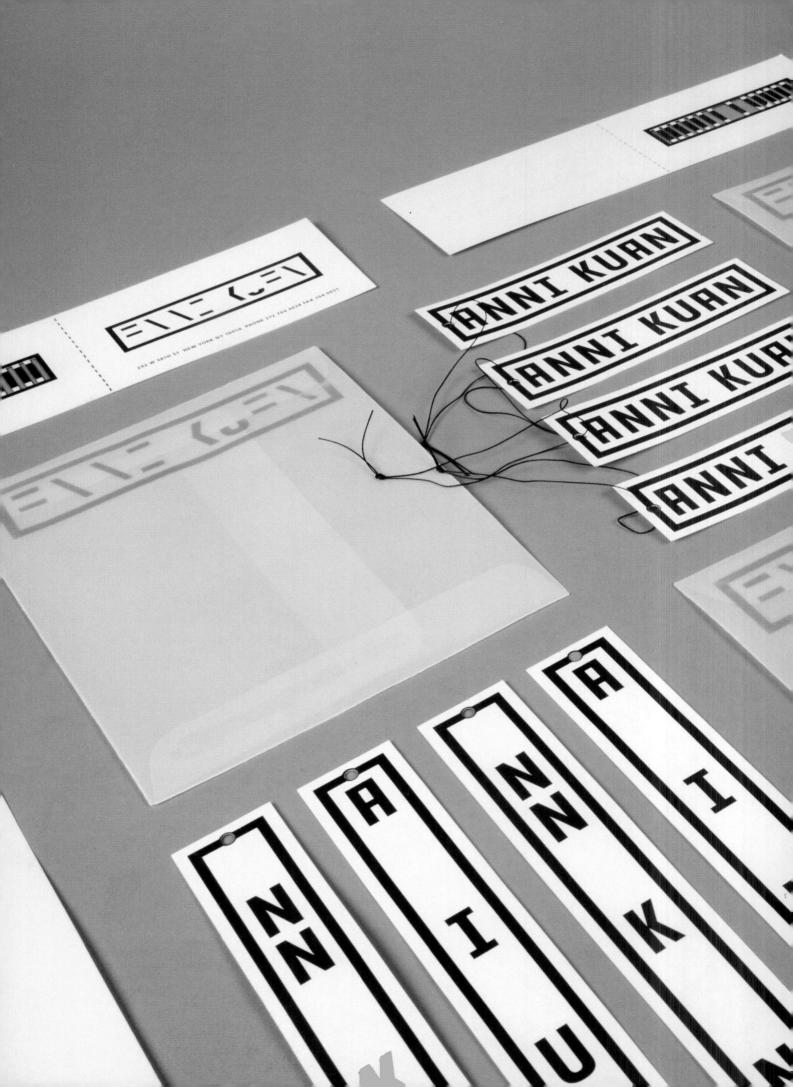

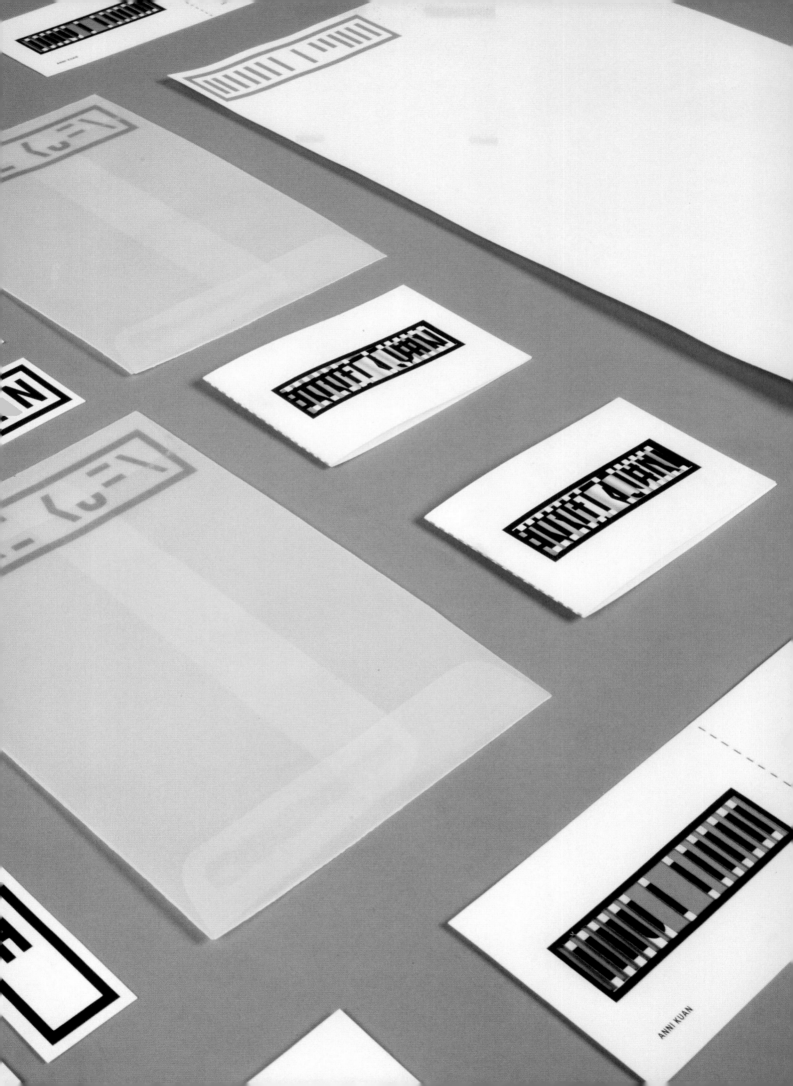

ANNI KUAN

[4] Anni Kuan business card

[5] Anni Kuan business card

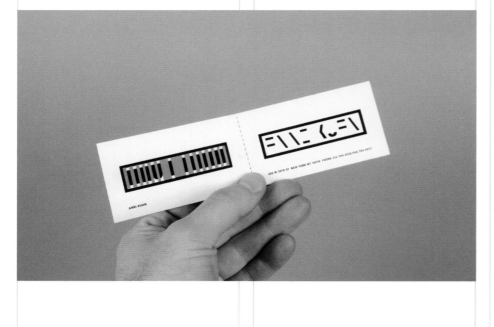

[1] James Long Menswear, marbling / paint / pencil, 2012

[2] Alexander McQueen, acrylic / paint, 2008

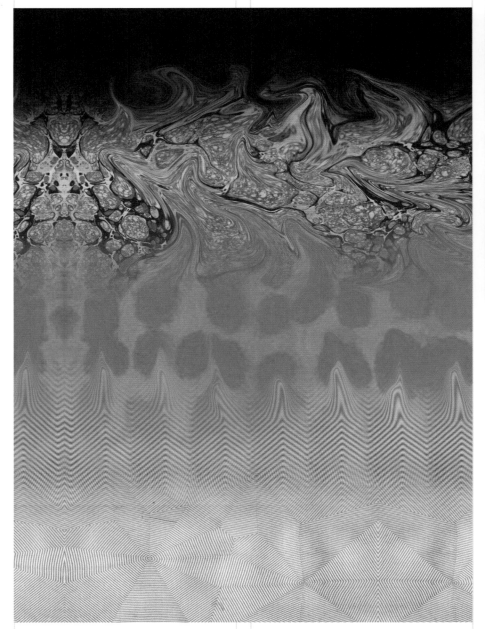

Seetal Solanki

Design
London, UK

Seetal Solanki is a London-based multidisciplinary design studio, delivering design, art and creative direction within the realms of fashion, wearable technology, sustainability, architecture, installations, materials, automotive, interiors, trend forecasting, research, strategy, brand identity, publications for print and online, and more. Seetal has spent the past ten years building on her style and unique approach to creative briefs and projects. Through her time of running her own studio she has gained an insight into working in a wide range of disciplines. She has the same approach when it comes to the creative process, and none of her work has the same outcome, as it will lend itself to a different result depending on what the idea is in the first place. She believes that the creative process shouldn't have an end result that is known from the beginning. There is a purpose to everything she creates, whether it be an artwork, a strong narrative, a visual identity or even just something great to look at.

Seetal graduated from Central Saint Martins with an MA in Design for Textile Futures. The studio collaborates with a number of industry experts, which allows it to achieve an international presence. Clients include Nike, Levi's Made & Crafted, Surface To Air, Alexander McQueen, Hussein Chalayan, Nissan Design Europe, It's Nice That, *Alvar* magazine, WGSN, Havaianas, United Visual Artists, PPQ, Markus Lupfer, Hentsch Man, Roland Mouret, Chloé, Missoni, Pucci, Alberta Ferretti and James Long.

[4] Alexander McQueen, acrylic / paint, 2008
(overleaf)

[6] Missoni, marbling, 2011

[7] Alexander McQueen, paint / Photoshop, 2012

[8] Alexander McQueen, paint / Photoshop, 2012

[9] Alexander McQueen, paint / Photoshop, 2008

[10] Missoni, marbling, 2011

[11] Alexander McQueen, paint / Photoshop, 2012

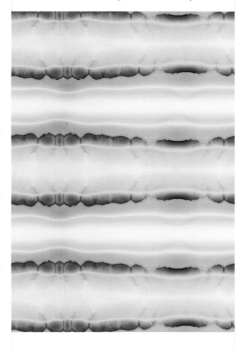

[1] 'This Peculiar Bias Will Nonetheless Set Up a Vast Field for the Unforeseen', installation including screen-printed paper, 2013

[2] 'This Peculiar Bias Will Nonetheless Set Up a Vast Field for the Unforeseen', installation including screen-printed paper, 2013

Seripop

Screen printing, installation, sculpture
Montreal, Canada

Yannick Desranleau and Chloe Lum have collaborated since 2000. Their work has been exhibited internationally, notably at the Blackwood Gallery (University of Toronto, 2012), Musée d'Art Contemporain de Montréal (Quebec Triennial 2011), Kunsthalle Wien (Vienna, Austria, 2010), BALTIC Centre for Contemporary Art (Gateshead, UK, 2009), Peacock Visual Arts (Aberdeen, UK, 2009) and Whitechapel Project Space (London, UK, 2007). Their work is in many private and public collections, notably the Victoria and Albert Museum in London.

Desranleau and Lum's work often takes the form of immersive installations and free-standing works that articulate themselves with the space they inhabit. This space, with its physical limits or arbitrary boundaries, and along with the materials specific to those works investing it, thus becomes a complete part of their visual syntax. As a result, site specificity is a common theme in the duo's works: either through unique interventions in reaction to a given space/area and context, or objectified as a module to which a work should adapt itself.

The installations have their origins in research the duo conducted on the subject of street posters, in order to understand their function as topographical markers and their relation with their physical and human environment. This research, once applied in the context of gallery installation, brought Desranleau and Lum to playfully engage in a formal game with the poster where the concepts of space, semantics and material durability are brought back into question. Through colour, the installations suggest new volumes or dramatize existing depths;

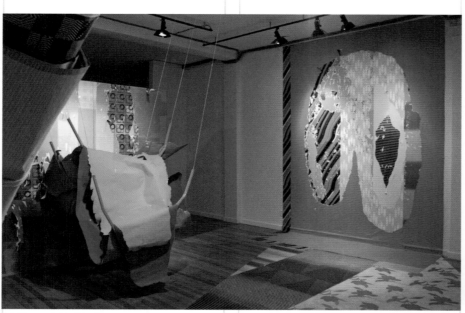

[4] 'Uncountable (Not Comparable)', installation, screen-printed paper, found wallpaper, string, wood, fabric, bricks, tempera, 2012

[5] 'The Options That Are Offered To Us: The Least Likely / The Most Tolerable', installation, screen-printed paper, 2012

[6] 'More Time than Space', installation, screen-printed paper, MDF, paint, lumber, rope, hooks, 2012

[7] 'What Should Have Been And What Would Not', installation, screen-printed paper, fishing net, anchors, 2012

[9] 'This Peculiar Bias Will Nonetheless Set Up a Vast Field for the Unforeseen', installation, 2013

[10] 'This Peculiar Bias Will Nonetheless Set Up a Vast Field for the Unforeseen', installation including screen-printed paper, 2013

by the use and misuse of screen-printed paper, the works create impressions of massiveness through the paradoxical manipulation and display of a delicate material; meaning gets subtracted or added by using typographic elements where form and function are informed by the street poster. The resulting works are not limited to a formal exploration within these media and concepts, as they carry multiple streams of thought that are simultaneously exposed within the work at different degrees of readability; an amalgamation of ideas that is issued from the ongoing discussion between the two artists.

[11] 'Uncountable (Not Comparable)', installation, screen-printed paper, found wallpaper, string, wood, fabric, bricks, tempera, 2012

[12] 'Uncountable (Not Comparable)', installation, screen-printed paper, found wallpaper, string, wood, fabric, bricks, tempera, 2012

[13] 'Uncountable (Not Comparable)', installation, screen-printed paper, found wallpaper, string, wood, fabric, bricks, tempera, 2012

[1] Folding Pictorial Field, screen print, 2013

Sonnenzimmer

Printmaking
Boston, Massachusetts, USA

Sonnenzimmer is the Chicago-based art studio of Nick Butcher and Nadine Nakanishi. Beginning as a shared painting studio in 2006, equipped with industrial screen-printing equipment, the endeavour quickly morphed into a graphic arts concern specializing in hand-crafted posters, music packaging and design work for some of Chicago's most recognizable cultural institutions, including the Chicago Symphony Orchestra, Newberry Library, Museum of Contemporary Art Chicago, and the Poetry Foundation. More recently, the duo have returned to the fine-art realm, mounting exhibits of their painting, textile and sound works in 2012 at the Minneapolis College of Art and Design and in 2013 at Public Works Gallery in Chicago. Their work has been published in books by Gestalten, Gingko Press, Pepin Press, Princeton Architectural Press and Rockport Publishers. Their poster work can be found in collections of the Art Institute of Chicago's Design and Architecture Department, the Museum of Design Zürich's Plakatraum and the University of Maryland's The Art Gallery. Their artist's books are also at home in Joan Flasch Artists' Book Collection at the School of the Art Institute of Chicago, Stanford University's Art and Architecture Library, and Vanderbilt University, to name a few.

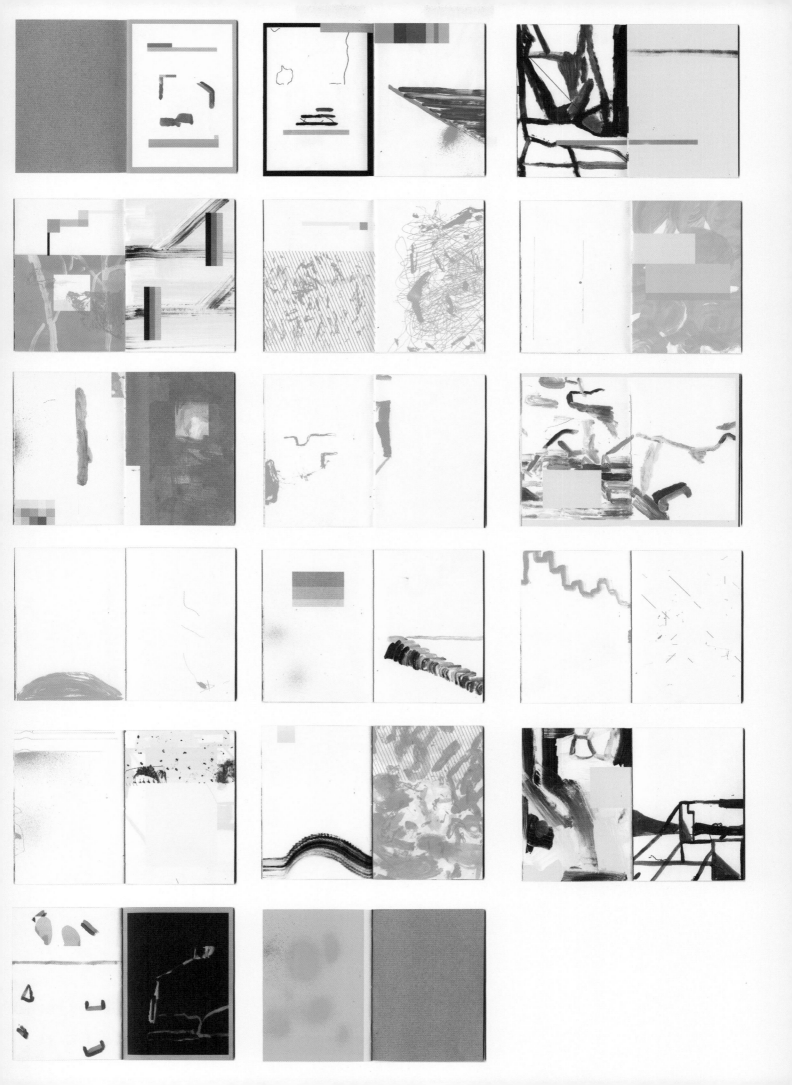

[4] Tim Hecker, Pitchfork Festival, screen print, 2012

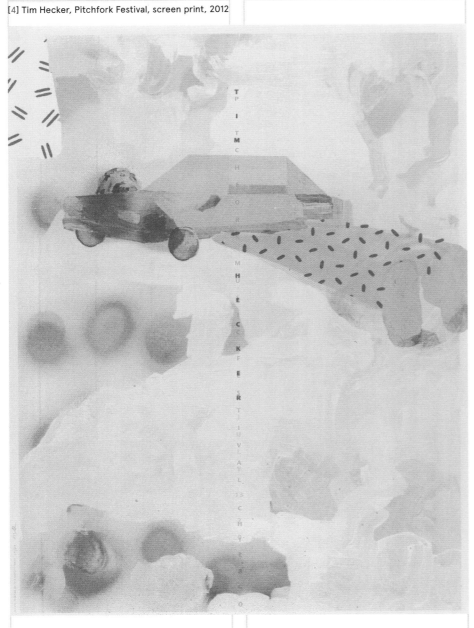

[5] Objet, screen print, 2012

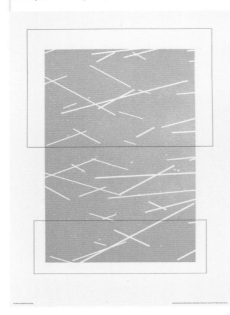

[6] Plastic Paper, screen print, 2010

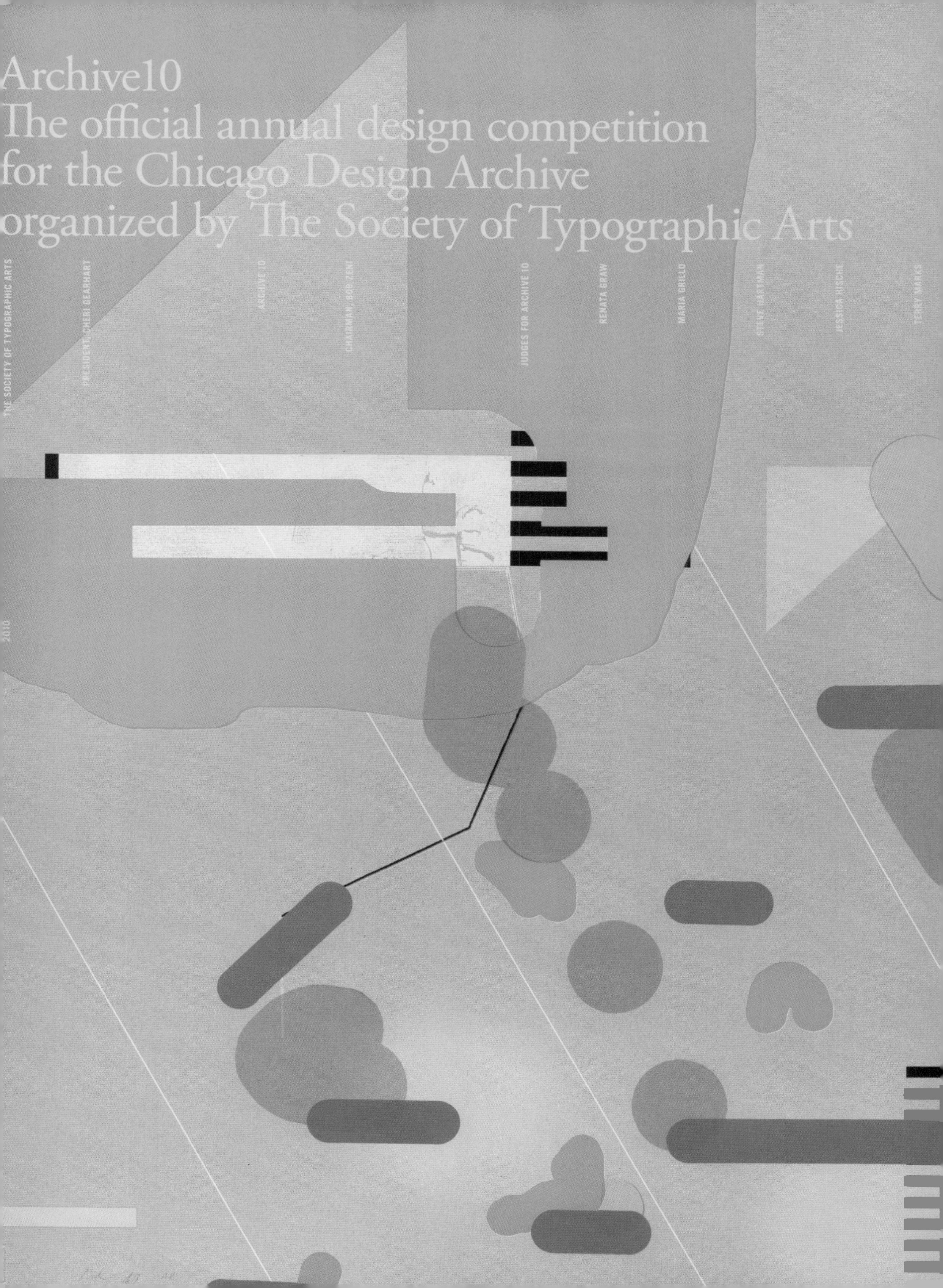

Archive 10
The official annual design competition
for the Chicago Design Archive
organized by The Society of Typographic Arts

THE SOCIETY OF TYPOGRAPHIC ARTS

PRESIDENT, CHERI GEARHART

ARCHIVE 10

CHAIRMAN, BOB ZEN

JUDGES FOR ARCHIVE 10

RENATA GRAW

MARIA GRILLO

STEVE HARTMAN

JESSICA HISCHE

TERRY MARKS

2010

[1] Studio set-up in Clapham, London

[2] Mixing inks for a limited-edition letterpress print

Studio Mothership

Graphic design
London, UK

Studio Mothership is a graphic design studio working on commissions from a wide range of creative organizations, educational institutions, artists, curators, companies and individuals from the cultural sector. Ken Borg and Lucy Sloss founded Studio Mothership while studying at the University for the Creative Arts in Farnham, Surrey. Ken is a graphic designer, while Lucy studied photography but found her ideal field of work in Web design and development. They came together to form the studio after collaborating on a number of university projects. Their combined knowledge and varied skills strengthened the collaboration and helped form the basis of their current studio practice. Creative output is varied, from print and Web-based projects to environmental design. The majority of their projects include identity work, way-finding, exhibition design, and editorial and layout, all of which reflect the duo's search for functional contemporary design. The work they produce reflects their admiration of modernist graphic design and Swiss principles. They describe their studio as a live-in workshop, one in which they spend most of their days. Their collaboration started off as a humble set-up in their rshared student house, and even though the location of their studio has changed they are still keen to describe it as their 'living space'. With Ken having a number of years of experience in print, and Lucy being an avid Web researcher, they revel in the

[4] Epsom Show invite, offset, 2013

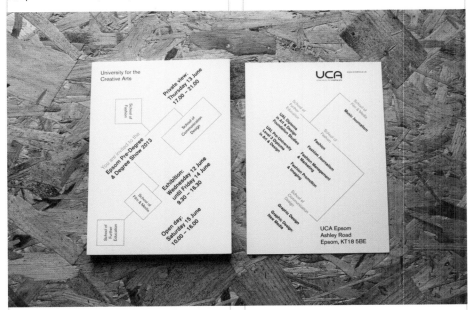

[5] Epsom way-finding signage, screen print, 2013

possibilities of influencing each other's practice to produce interesting outcomes, which share cross-platform principles. Their process is solidly research-based and although the practice sees just the two of them manning the studio with occasional placement assistants, tasks and responsibilities are shared mand assigned individually. They emphasize how important it is to have a sound structure to the business and how having dedicated roles is vital to the smooth running of the studio and of each project the studio takes on. They say they always admired the small studio model, which gives the designer the possibility to get involved in any stage of the business, from the administration to dealing directly with client accounts and sourcing new work. Ken and Lucy say that their vision is not necessarily seeing the studio increase in size, but that they are keen to make sure their practice remains true to the roots that formed it, with a small team working together and getting involved in every project. The most important thing to them is to constantly manage the balance between all the media and processes they use. They are avid researchers of new technologies and new possibilities for applying ideas to a project effectively, but at the same time they are keen to keep to the core principles of print techniques, materials used and typesetting. This is evident in their use of traditional processes such as letterpress, which is alive in much of their print-based work, both commercial and studio projects. They also occasionally host and run live letterpress print workshops at their London-based studio and at events.

[6] Bread & Roses Film Festival, risograph, 2012

[7] Bread & Roses Film Festival, risograph, 2012

[8] Muster Print, letterpress, 2011

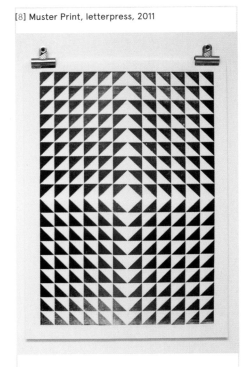

[9] Open Studio Weekend, offset, 2013

[10] For Future Reference, offset, 2013

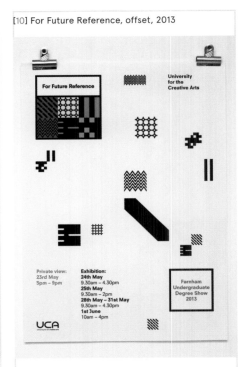

[11] Made Show, offset, 2012

[12] Bread & Roses Film Festival, offset, 2012

[13] Bookroom Workshop Series, screen print, 2011

[14] Hampshire Map, risograph, 2013

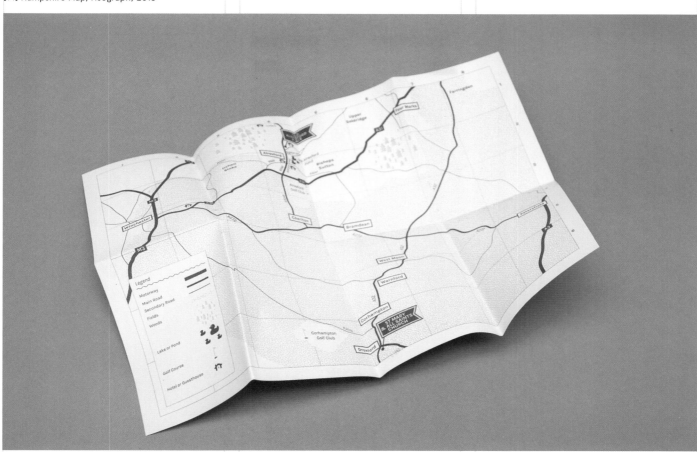

[15] The Book is Alive!, offset, 2013

[1] Strolling, 2014

[2] Working, 2014

Team Print Shop

Printmaking
Oakland, California, USA

Founded by John O. Ream IV, Team Print Shop is a full-service creative and technical shop with both designers and printers on staff. Team Print Shop is located in Oakland, California, and has formed a niche in design, print and the exclusive community of travelling bicycle print shops.

Before venturing to the West Coast, Ream spent his formative years in Pennsylvania drawing images of landscapes with blueberry suns and dreaming of one day owning a scrap-metal recycling empire. As a college student,

these creative/industrious rustbelt aspirations translated to a curriculum focusing as much on the theory of graphic design as on the practical implementation of printmaking. Upon graduation, Ream found employment in shops fostering both his creative and his technical capabilities.

Ream's experiences as a designer and printer resulted in the establishment of a print shop acknowledging both the technical implementation of design and the art of print. Influenced by creative forces such as Andy Warhol and Don

Rickles, Team Print Shop caters to a diverse demographic ranging from your favourite neighbourhood bar to the San Francisco Museum of Modern Art to the loan shark you would prefer to not acknowledge among colleagues.

[5] Mixing, 2014

[6] Mixing, 2014

[7] Betty the Press, 2014

[1] Garden, woodcut, 2012

Tugboat Printshop

Printmaking
Pittsburgh, Pennsylvania, USA

Paul Roden and Valerie Lueth are the collaborative woodcut artists known as Tugboat Printshop. The couple have been publishing their traditionally hand-crafted colour woodblock print editions from Pittsburgh, Pennsylvania, since 2006. Tugboat Printshop's intricate colour woodcuts celebrate the natural world and humankind's relationship to it. With extreme focus on craft and detail, the artists build idealistic, nostalgic and meticulously patterned worlds with their traditionally made prints. Rich colour is layered in multiple impressions from hand-drawn, hand-carved and individually printed wood blocks. All prints are published with top-shelf oil-based inks on to fine papers. Tugboat Printshop's narrative is one of sustainability, resourcefulness and an upbeat do-good attitude.

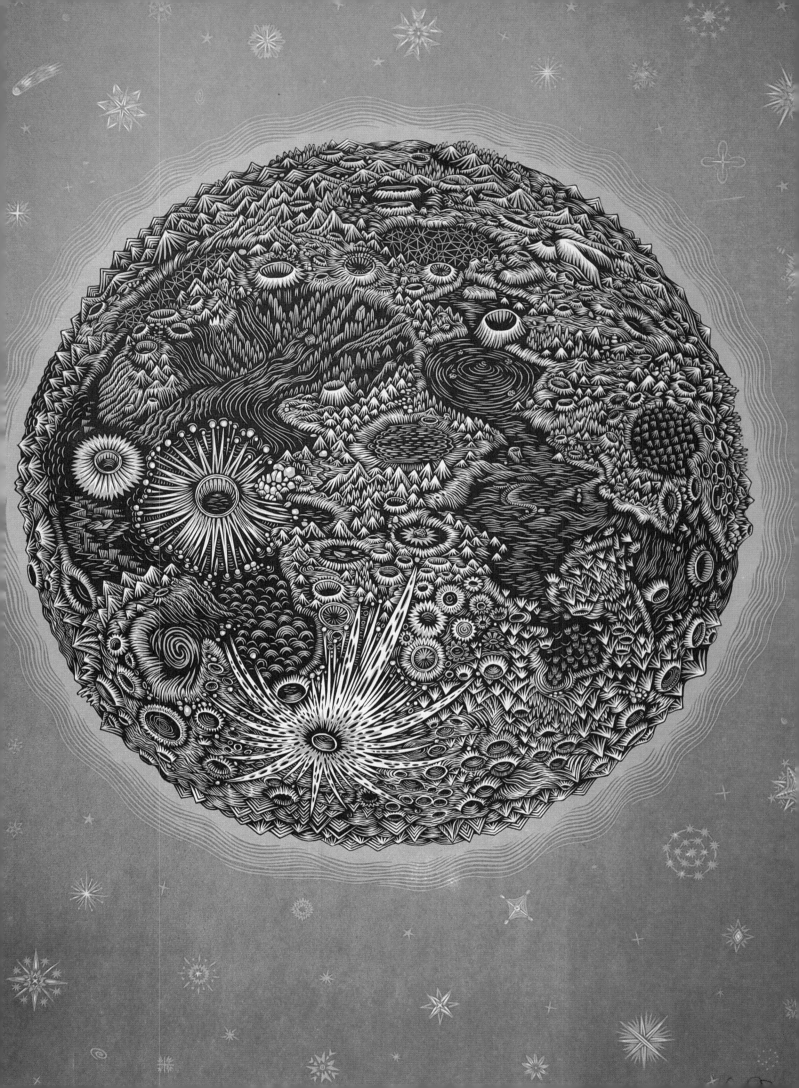

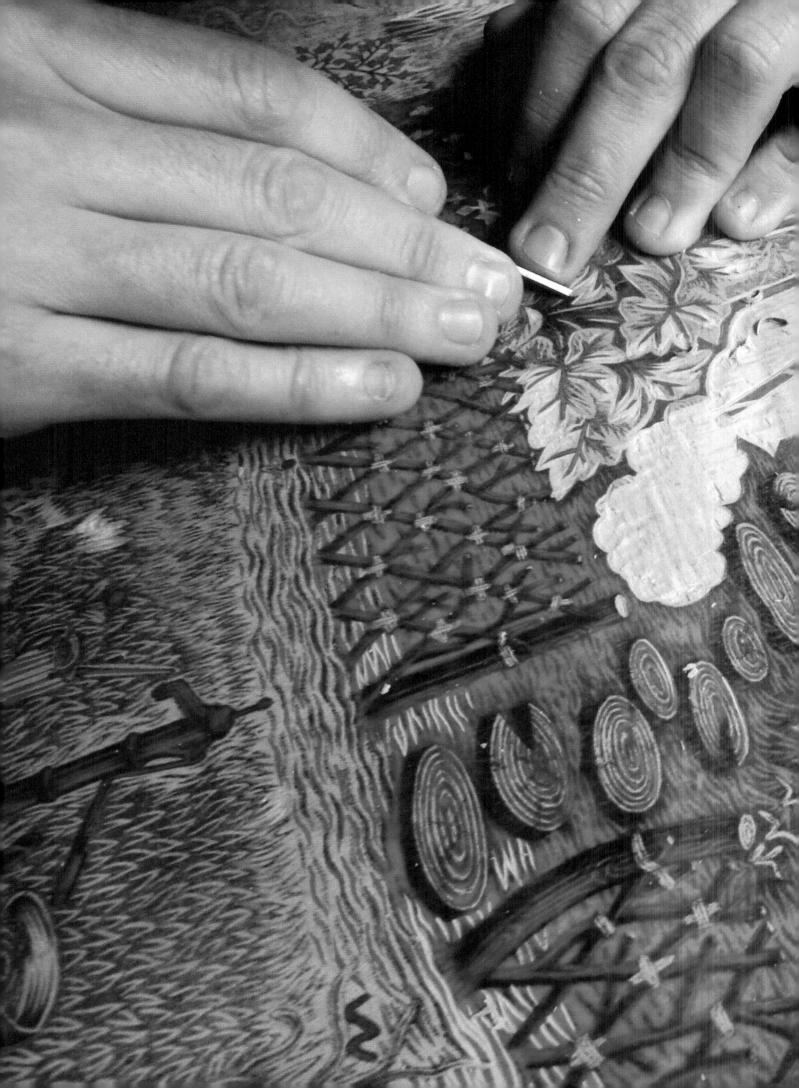

[4] Desert Island, woodcut, 2014

[5] Moon, woodcut, 2012

[6] Clod, woodcut, 2012

Part 3: **Directory** – a selection of print-based websites
Index
Credits

# #

1/1 — Italy
Letterpress — uno-di-uno.com

1/2 — France
Artists/graphic designers — undemi.fr

10 Deep — USA
Streetwear brand — 10deep.com

3939 Shop — UK
Retail outlet — 3939shop.com

A

A G Magee — UK
Screen printer — agmagee.tumblr.com

A is a name — France
Graphic designer — a-is-a.name

Aarin Smith — Canada
Photographer — aarinsmith.com

Adam Bletchly — UK
Illustrator — adambletch.com

Adam Friedman — USA
Painter/artist — artbyadamfriedman.com

Adam Hancher — UK
Illustrator — adamhancher.co.uk

Adeline Meilliez — Germany
Visual artist — adelinemeilliez.com

Aekido — UK
Graphic designer — thisisaekido.co.uk

Aesthetic Apparatus — USA
Printmaker — aestheticapparatus.com

Aesthetica — UK
Culture magazine — aestheticamagazine.com

Age of Reason — UK
Accessories brand — age-of-reason-studios.com

Alakazam — UK
Creative outlet — alakazamlabel.com

Alessandra Genualdo — UK
Illustrator — cargocollective.com/agenualdo

Alex Fakso — UK
Photographer — fakso.com

Alex Mathers — UK
Illustrator — alexmathers.net

Alex May Hughes — UK
Artist — alexmayhughes.co.uk

Alex Trochut — Spain
Graphic designer/illustrator — alextrochut.com

Alice Potter — UK
Graphic designer/illustrator — alicepotter.co.uk

Alice Tye — UK
Illustrator — cargocollective.com/alicetye

Amanda Greenberg — USA
Illustrator — amanda-greenberg.com

Amelia Hall — USA
Graphic designer — ameliahall.com

Amy Louise Olszak — UK
Illustrator — cargocollective.com/amyolszak

An Endless Supply — UK
Graphic designer — anendlesssupply.co.uk

Ana Schefer — UK
Graphic designer — anaschefer.com

Andrew Berwick — UK
Illustrator/printmaker — andrewberwick.co.uk

Andrew Holder — USA
Graphic designer/illustrator — andrewholder.net

Andy Cooke — UK
Graphic designer — thisisandycooke.com

Andy Seize — UK
Artist — andyseize.co.uk

Andy Smith — UK
Illustrator — asmithillustration.com

Angela Dalinger — Germany
Artist — angeladalinger.tumblr.com

Angus MacKenzie — UK
Screen printer — angusmackenzie.co.uk

Ann-Marie Rayney — UK
Fine artist — cargocollective.com/annmarierayney

Antenne Books — UK
Publisher — antennebooks.com

Anthem SF — USA
Screen printer — anthemprintingsf.com

Anthony Burrill — UK
Graphic artist — anthonyburrill.com

Apenest — USA
Printmaker/publisher — apenest.com

Art & Sole — UK
Retailer — artandsoleblog.com

Art Paper Editions — Belgium
Publisher — artpapereditions.org

Artizan Editions — UK
Screen printer — artizaneditions.co.uk

Ashkahn Shahparnia — USA
Artist/designer — ashkahn.com

Ashton Screen Print — UK
Screen printer — ashtonscreenprint.com

Aurelia Lange — UK
Illustrator/printmaker — aurelialange.co.uk

B

BAM — UK
Design label — bambooteak.com

Bare Bones — UK
Publisher — ourbarebones.co.uk

Barney McCann — UK
Photographer — barneymccann.com

Bas Koopmans — The Netherlands
Graphic designer — baster.nl

Basso and Brooke — UK
Printer/designer — bassoandbrooke.com

Beach London — UK
Café/bookshop/gallery — beachlondon.co.uk

Beatriz Sanches — UK
Graphic designer/illustrator — beatrizsanches.com

Beautiful/Decay — USA
Art/book — beautifuldecay.com

Becca Allen — UK
Graphic designer/illustrator — beccaallen.co.uk

Bedford Press — UK
Publisher — bedfordpress.org

Bellevue Press — UK
Risograph printer — bellevuepress.blogspot.co.uk

Ben Newman — UK
Illustrator/art director — bennewman.co.uk

Beniffer Editions — Canada
Art music record label — beniffereditions.com

Benjamin C. Carr — UK
Graphic designer/illustrator — benjamincarr.com

Benjamin Nelson — UK
Graphic designer — bnelsonartdesign.blogspot.co.uk

Benjamin Woodcock — UK
Illustrator — cargocollective.com/benjaminwoodcock

Beyond Thrilled Screenprints & Illustration — UK
Illustrator/screen printer — beyondthrilled.com

Bjørn Rune Lie — UK
Illustrator — bjornlie.com

Black + White + Colour — UK
Graphic designer — blackandwhiteandcolour.co.uk

Black Box Press — UK
Publisher — blackboxpress.co.uk

Black Rat Projects and Press — UK
Career support — blackratprojects.com

Blim — Canada
Art and craft facility — blim.ca

Blush — UK
Letterpress — blushpublishing.co.uk

Bob Eight Pop — UK
Screen printer — bobeightpop.com

Bolo Paper — Italy
Publisher — bolopaper.com

Bolt Editions — UK
Risograph printer — bolteditions.co.uk

Booklyn — USA
Artist/bookmakers — booklyn.org

BPW — UK
Print workshop/charity — bpw.org.uk

Bradley Jay — UK
Illustrator — bradleyjay.co.uk

Brainrental — Hong Kong
Illustrator — facebook.com/brainrental

Brigid Deacon (NSFW) — UK
Illustrator — brigiddeacon.com

Broken Fingaz — Israel
Graffiti artists — brokenfingaz.com

Bronze Age — UK
Publisher — bronze-age.net

Burgerac — UK
Burger-related products — burgerac.com

Burlesque of North America — USA
Graphic designer — burlesquedesign.com

C

C-Heads — Austria
Magazine — c-heads.com

Calm & Collected — UK
Creative studio — wearecalmandcollected.com

Calverts — UK
Designer/printer — calverts.coop

Catalogue Libray — UK
Publisher — thisiscatalogue.co.uk

Caz Haigh — UK
Graphic designer/illustrator — cazhaigh.co.uk

Charlotte Hall — UK
Printmaker — eccentrichorace.blogspot.co.uk

Charlotte-Maëva Perret — UK
Designer — cargocollective.com/brandnewpixel

Cherelle Sappleton — UK
Artist/photographer — cherellesappleton.tumblr.com

Chris Magnusson — Sweden
Artist/animator — rwealone.eu

Chris Mercier — UK
Artist/printmaker — chrismercier.co.uk

Claire Heffer Design — UK
Designer/writer/photographer — claireheffer.com

Clerk Ink Well — UK
Letterpress — clerkinkwell.com

CMRTYZ — USA
Art/fashion/music — cmrtyz.com

Coal Shed Press — UK
Linocut/woodcut/etching — coalshedpress.co.uk

Colophon — UK
Type foundry — colophon-foundry.org

Colour Code — Canada
Publisher/printer — colourcodeprinting.com

Comet Substance — Switzerland
Graphic artist — cometsubstance.com

Concrete Hermit — UK
Retail outlet — concretehermit.com

Corrupiola — Brazil
Illustrator/printmaker — corrupiola.com.br

Crafty Fox Market — UK
Craft market — craftyfoxmarket.co.uk

Cryptogram Ink — USA
Graphic designer/printmaker — cryptogramink.com

D

Daisy Whitehouse — UK
Illustrator — whitewolfillustrations.com

Damien Poulain — UK
Graphic designer — damienpoulain.com

Dan Baldwin — UK
Artist — danbaldwinart.com

Dan Hillier — UK
Illustrator — danhillier.com

Dan Mumford — UK
Illustrator/printmaker — dan-mumford.com

Dana McClure — USA
Printmaker — danamcclure.com

Daniel Fletcher — UK
Graphic designer — cargocollective.com/danielfletcher

Danielle Louise Watt — UK
Illustrator/printmaker — daniellewatt.com

Dave Bain — UK
Illustrator — davebain.com

David Foldvari — UK
Illustrator — davidfoldvari.co.uk

David Pearson — UK
Graphic designer — typeasimage.com

David Saunders — UK
Fine artsist — daviddavidlondon.tumblr.com

Day Zine — UK
Publisher — dayzine.co.uk

Dean Brierley/Sodastream — UK
Artist — dean-brierley.blogspot.co.uk

Designers & Books — USA
Publisher — designersandbooks.com

Diego Mena — UK
Artist — didacus.co.uk

Dionne Kitching — UK
Illustrator/printmaker — dionnekitching.co.uk

Doe Eyed — USA
Printmaker — doe-eyed.com

Dogboy — UK
Illustator/printmaker — dogboy.co

Don't be Shy — Argentina
Publisher — dontbeshy.com.ar

Donuts The Store — UK
Store — donutsthestore.co.uk

Dooom — UK
Illustrator — iamdooom.com

Drawn in Bristol — UK
Illustrator — drawninbristol.co.uk

Drink, Shop & Do — UK
Café/bar/shop — drinkshopdo.com

Drop Dead Clothing — UK
Store — iheartdropdead.com

Duet Letterpress — UK
Letterpress — duetletterpress.com

E

East London Printmakers — UK
Printmaker — eastlondonprintmakers.co.uk

Ed J Brown — UK
Illustrator — edjbrown.com

Eimearjean McCormack — UK, France, China
Printmaker — eimearjean.blogspot.com

Eleanor Lines — UK
Artist — eleanorlines.com

Elizabeth Corkery — USA
Printmaker — elizabethcorkery.com

Elizabeth Walker — UK
Printmaker — elizabethwalker.co.uk

Elizabeth Warmisham — UK
Photographer — elizabethwarmisham.com

Ella Barrett — UK
Print designer — ellabarrett.co.uk

Emily Forgot — UK
Graphic artist — emilyforgot.co.uk

Emine Ortega — USA
Surface pattern — emineortega.blogspot.com

Emma Shipley — UK
Illustrator/fashion — emmajshipley.com

Entrepreneurs — UK
Store — ntrprnrs.com

Erik Winkowski — USA
Graphic artist — erikwinkowski.com

Ever Loving Press — USA
Letterpress — everlovinpress.tumblr.com

EyeBall Comix — UK
Comic bookshop — eyeballcomix.co.uk

F

Fatherless — USA
Print collective — wearefatherless.com

Fikra — UAE
Design studio — fikradesigns.com

Finn O'Brien — UK
Printmaker/designer — finn-obrien.com

Flamingo Arts Project — UK
Publisher — flamingomagazine.com

Florence Shaw — UK
Illustrator/writer — florenceshaw.com

French — UK
Illustrator — funeralfrench.com

Freshly Pressed Printing — USA
Printmaker — freshlypressedprinting.com

Frinton Press — UK
Printmaker — cargocollective.com/frintonpress

G

Gabriela Szulman — UK
Printmaker — gabrielaszulman.com

Garret Karol — USA
Graphic designer — garrettkarol.com

Garudio Studiage — UK
Creative collective — garudiostudiage.com

Gem Copeland — The Netherlands
Designer — gemcopeland.com

Gemma Land — UK
Visual artist — gemmaland.com

Generation Press — UK
Printer — generationpress.co.uk

Get a Grip — UK
Printmaker — getagripstudio.com

Gina Baber — UK
Printmaker/artist — ginababer.com

Glasgow Press — UK
Letterpress — glasgowpress.com

Good Press Gallery — UK
Gallery/shop — goodpressgallery.co.uk

Grady Gordon — USA
Artist — gradygordon.com

Graphic Exchange — UK
Designer — graphic-exchange.com

Guerilla Print — Germany
Printmaker — facebook.com/guerilla.print

Gunsho — USA
Illustrator — scuzzdemon.blogspot.com

H

Handmade Posters — Norway
Printmaker — handmadeposters.com

Handprinted — UK
Screen printer — handprinted.co.uk

Hannah Buck — UK
Illustrator/printmaker — missbuck.com

Hannah Waldron — UK
Artist/design — hannahwaldron.co.uk

Harriet Alana — UK
Illustrator — harrietalana.co.uk

Harry Diaz — USA
Illustrator/printmaker — harrydiaz.com

Hato Press — UK
Printmaker — hatopress.net

Heather Huston — USA
Artist — hhuston.com

Hell'O Monsters — Belguim
Collective — hellomonsters.wordpress.com

Hello Dodo — UK
Screen printer — hello-dodo.blogspot.co.uk

HERE Gallery — UK
Gallery — thingsfromhere.co.uk/gallery

Heretic — UK
Printmaker — hereticprintmakers.blogspot.com

Heuberger — UK
Print collective — heubergercentral.blogspot.co.uk

Hippo Screenprinters — UK
Screen printer — hipposcreenprinters.com

Holly Bagnall — UK
Graphic designer — cargocollective.com/hollybagnall

Holly Drewett — UK
Printmaker — hollydrewett.com

Holly Exley —UK
Illustrator — hollyexley.com

Hot Bed Press — UK
Printmaker — hotbedpress.org

Hugh Barrell — UK
Printmaker — cargocollective.com/hughbarrell

I

I Dress Myself — UK
Screen printer — idressmyself.co.uk

Iain Mckell — UK
Photographer — iainmckell.com

Ian Stevenson — UK
Illustrator — ianstevenson.co.uk

Icon Printing — UK
Printmaker — iconprinting.com

Idem Paris — France
Printmaker — idemparis.com

Ill-Studio — France
Graphic designer — ill-studio.com

Illustrated People — UK
Fashion collective — illustratedpeople.com

Inc. Zine — UK
Publisher — inc-zine.blogspot.co.uk

indcsn — UK
Clothing brand — indcsn.com

Ink and Thread — UK
Store — inkandthread.co.uk

INKwell Print — UK
Screen printer — inkwellprint.co.uk

Inky Solutions — UK
Print-management company — inkysolutions.com

Inkygoodness — UK
Blog — inkygoodness.com

J

Intaglio — UK
Printmaker — intaglioprintmaker.com

Invisible Industries — USA
Online shop — invisible-industries.com

Isle of Printing — USA
Printmaker — isleofprinting.com

Issey Miyake — Japan
Designer — isseymiyake.com/en

Iwona Przybyla — Poland
Graphic designer — iwonaprzybyla.com

Jack Hudson — UK
Graphic designer/illustrator — jack-hudson.com

Jack Sachs — UK
Animator/illustrator — jacksachs.co.uk

Jake Blanchard — UK
Illustrator — jakeblanchard.co.uk

James Brown — UK
Printmaker/illustrator — generalpattern.net

James Dicks — UK
Illustrator — jamesdicks.co.uk

James Jessiman — UK
Printmaker — jamesjessiman.com

Jamie Mills — UK
Illustrator — jamiemillsillustration.blogspot.co.uk

Janne Iivonen — UK
Illustrator — janneiivonen.net

Jasper Goodall — UK
Illustrator — jaspergoodall.com

Jealous Gallery — UK
Gallery — jealousgallery.com

Jean-Pierre Raynaud — France
Artist — jeanpierreraynaud.com

Jefferson Cheng — USA
Designer/illustrator — jeffersoncheng.com

Jennie Webber — UK
Illustrator — jenniewebber.com

Jeremyville — USA, Australia
Artist — jeremyville.com

Jesse Tise — USA
Illustrator — ofgodsandmonsters.net

Jessica Hische — USA
Graphic designer — jessicahische.is/awesome

Jessie May Bennett — UK
Printmaker — jessiemaybennett.blogspot.co.uk

Jez Burrows — UK
Designer/illustrator — jezburrows.com

Jim Stoten — UK
Illustrator — jimtheillustrator.co.uk

Jimmy Turrell — UK
Illustrator — jimmyturrell.blogspot.co.uk

Jiro Bevis — UK
Illustrator — jirobevis.co.uk

Jo Stafford — UK
Printmaker — jostaffordjostafford.blogspot.com

Joe Cruz — UK
Textile designer — jcruz.co.uk

Joe Snow — UK
Printmaker/illustrator — joesnow.co.uk

John C Thurbin — UK
Printmaker — cargocollective.com/johncthurbin

Johnny Sampson — USA
Artist — johnnysampson.com

Jon Boam — UK
Artist — cargocollective.com/jonboam

Jon Burgerman — UK
Illustrator — jonburgerman.com

Jon Ford — UK
Graphic designer/illustrator — jfgd.co.uk

Jon Vermilyea — USA
Printmaker — jonvermilyea.com

Jonna Saarinen — Finland
Textile designer — jonnasaarinen.com

Jordan Andrew Carter — UK
Illustrator — jordanandrewcarter.co.uk

Joseph Vass — UK
Illustrator/printmaker — josephvass.com

Josephine Hicks — UK
Illustrator/printmaker — josephinehicks.com

Joshua Hibbert — UK
Illustrator — joshuahibbert.blogspot.co.uk
Josie Falconer — UK
Graphic designer — josiefalconer.com

Julia Corsaro — UK
Photographer — juliacorsaro.com

Jungyeon Roh — USA
Illustrator — jungyeonroh.com

justAjar — USA
Design press — justajar.com

Justyna Michalowska — UK
Textile designer — justynamichalowska.co.uk

K

K2 Screen — UK
Screen printer — k2screen.co.uk

Kaput — Brazil
Publisher — kaputlivros.com

Karl Grandin — Sweden
Graphic designer — karlgrandin.com

Kat Libretto — UK
Graphic designer — cargocollective.com/katlibretto

Kate Clift — UK
Graphic designer — kateclift.co.uk

Kate Prior — UK
Designer — kateprior.com

Katie Eleanor — UK
Photographic artist — katieeleanor.com

Katie Whitton — UK
Textile designer — katiewhitton.com

Katy Binks — UK
Artist/designer/screen printer — katybinks.tumblr.com

Katy Goutefangea — UK
Printmaker — katygoutefangea.com

Kayrock — USA
Screen printer — kayrock.org

Keegan Meegan & Co. — USA
Letterpress — keeganmeeganco.com

Kerr Vernon — UK
Graphic designer — kerrvernon.co.uk

Kieron Lewis — UK
Graphic designer — kieronlewis.com

Killer Acid — USA
Illustrator — killeracid.com

Kim Sielbeck — USA
Printmaker — kimsielbeck.com

Kings Framers — UK
Framers — kingsframers.com

Kitty Joseph — UK
Textile designer — kittyjoseph.com

Kraggy — UK
Illustrator — kraggy.co.uk

L

L_A_N — USA
Magazine — lanzine.com

Landland — USA
Graphic designer/illustrator — landland.net

Laura Barnes — UK
Illustrator/textile designer — laurabarnes.co.uk

Laura Pannack — UK
Photographer — laurapannack.com

Lazy Oaf — UK
Store — lazyoaf.co.uk

Le Gun — UK
Creative collective — legun.co.uk

Leah V Wishnia — USA
Printmaker/illustrator — thespithouse.tumblr.com

Lennart Wolfert — The Netherlands
Graphic artist — lennartwolfert.nl

Les Tontons Racleurs — Belguim
Printmaker — lestontonsracleurs.be

Lesser Gonzalez Alvarez — USA
Illustrator — lessergonzalezalvarez.com

Liam Ashley Clark — UK
Fine artist — liamashleyclark.com

Lian Benoit — USA
Graphic designer — marecettepourunbondesign.ca

Lik + Neon — UK
Store — likneon.com

Linocut Boy — UK
Artist/illustrator — linocutboy.com

Linus Kraemer — UK
Graphic designer/illustrator — linuskraemer.com

Liquorice Press — UK
Printmaker — theliquoricegroup.co.uk

Lives & Levels Skateboard Co. — UK
Skateboarding company — livesandlevels.com

Lo Parkin — UK
Illustrator — loparkin.com

Logan Hicks — USA
Street artist — workhorsevisuals.com

Loligo — UK
Printmaker — loligo.org

London Centre for Book Arts — UK
Educational centre — londonbookarts.tumblr.com

London Graphic Centre — UK
Store — londongraphics.co.uk

London Print Studio — UK
Printmaker — londonprintstudio.org.uk

Long Muzzle — USA
Illustrator/printmaker — longmuzzle.com

Lost Studio — UK
Graphic designer/illustrator — loststudio.co.uk

Louise Lockhart — UK
Illustrator — theprintedpeanut.co.uk

Lovenskate — UK
Skateboarding company — lovenskate.com

Lucy K — UK
Illustrator — cargocollective.com/lucyk

Luis Toledo — Spain
Artist — laprisamata.es

Lynnie Zulu — UK
Illustrator — lynniezulu.tumblr.com

M

Make Away — UK
Creative business development — make-away.com

Man Up Girl! Ltd — UK
Clothing brand — manupgirl.com

Manchester Print Fair — UK
Print fair — manchesterprintfair.co.uk

Mansi Shah — USA
Illustrator — mansishah.com

Manuel Fernández — Spain
Artist — manuelfernandez.name

Marc the Printers — UK
Printer — marctheprinters.co.uk

Marcel Christ — The Netherlands
Photographer — marcelchrist.com

Marcel Cowling — UK
Artist — marcelcowling.co.uk

Marcroy Smith — UK
Graphic designer/printmaker — marcroy.co.uk

MaricorMaricar — Australia
Illustrator — maricormaricar.com

Mark Long — UK
Illustrator — marklongillustration.co.uk

Markus Haala — USA
Printmaker — mhaala.com

Markus Kaesler — Germany
Photographer — markuskaesler.de

MaryMe-JimmyPaul — The Netherlands
Fine artist — maryme-jimmypaul.com

Matt Lyon — UK
Illustrator — c8six.com

Matt Manson — UK
Surface pattern designer — mattmanson.co.uk

Matt Taylor — UK
Illustrator/comic artist — matttaylor.co.uk

Matthew Dayler — USA
Artist/printmaker — matthewdayler.com

Matthew Haysom — UK
Designer — matthewhaysom.co.uk

Mesh Collective — UK
Printmaker — mesh-collective.blogspot.com

Micah Lidberg — USA
Artist/illustrator — micahlidberg.com

Michael Arnold — UK
Illustrator — mkrnld.co.uk

Michael Chase — USA
Visual artist — areaofinterest.com

Michael Lester — UK
Designer/illustrator — michaelwilliamlester.com

Michael Mercer Brown — UK
Graphic designer — michaelmercerbrown.com

Michael van Kekem — The Netherlands
Illustrator/printmaker — michaelvankekem.com

Michael Willis — UK
Graphic artist — mwillis.eu

Michael Wolf — Hong Kong
Photographer — photomichaelwolf.com

Mikaela Lilhops — UK
Graphic designer/illustrator — mish.sk

Mike Perry — USA
Designer/artist — mikeperrystudio.com

Mike Zimmerman — USA
Designer — mike-zimmerman.com

Mimi Mollica — UK
Photographer/artist — mimimollica.com

Mina Bach — UK
Design student/printmaker — minabach.co.uk

Miranda Foxx — UK
Image maker — cargocollective.com/mirandafoxx

Miso — Australia
Street artist — m-i-s-o.com

Modern Giant Design — USA
Graphic designer — moderngiantdesign.com

Mojoko — Singapore
Graphic designer/artist/curator — mojoko.net

Molly Rooke — UK
Artist — mollyrooke.com

Moss — USA
Streetwear brand — mossclothing.com

Mr Gresty — UK
Designer/illustrator/curator — mrgresty.com

Mr PS — UK
Store — shop.mr-ps.co.uk

N

Nadine Tropschuh — UK
Artist — cargocollective.com/nadinetropschuh

Nathen Atia (NSFW) — UK
Photographer — nathenatia.com

NCC — UK
Design and print studio — neasdencontrolcentre.com

Newspaper Club — UK
Publisher — newspaperclub.com

Nic Bennett — UK
Graphic designer/printmaker — nicbennett.com

Nic Farrell — UK
Illustrator — nicfarrell.com

Nick Greenbank — UK
Designer — cargocollective.com/nickgreenbank

Nick Mattan — Belgium
Graphic designer — nickmattan.tumblr.com

Nick Sheehy — UK
Artist/illustrator — showchicken.com

Niklas Roy — Germany
Artist — niklasroy.com

No Guts No Glory — UK
Artist network — ngngdesign.com

Nobrow — UK
Publisher — nobrow.net

Noga Berman — Israel
Designer — nogaberman.com

Now What? — USA
Art collective — nowwhatposters.wordpress.com

NY Prisoner 63906054 — USA
Artist — newyorkprisoner63906054.blogspot.co.uk

O

OFF LIFE — UK
Street-press comic — offlife.co.uk

Oh, Snap! Project — USA
Photography project — theohsnapproject.com

Oliver Binnian — UK
Artist/designer — binnian.com

Olly Moss — UK
Graphic designer — ollymoss.com

Only More Never Less — USA
Graphic designer — onlymoreneverless.com

Ornamental Conifer — UK
Sign painter — ornamentalconifer.blogspot.co.uk

Oskar Kron — UK
Graphic designer — oskarkron.com

Outline Editions — UK
Outlet — outline-editions.co.uk

Owen Davey — UK
Illustrator — owendavey.com

Own Art — UK
Art retailer — ownart.org.uk

OWT — UK
Design collective — owtcreative.com

P

P.A.M — Australia
Fashion label — perksandmini.com

Pablo Abad — Spain
Graphic designer/art director — pabloabad.com

Palefroi — Germany
Art project/screen-print studio — palefroi.net

Part & Parcel — USA
Graphic designer — partparcelny.com

Patch D Keyes — UK
Illustrator/printmaker — patchdkeyes.co.uk

Patrick Savile — UK
Image maker/designer — patricksavile.com

Paul Blow — UK
Illustrator — paulblow.com

Paul Kelly — UK
Designer/illustrator — designbypaulkelly.com

Paul Price — UK
Designer/illustrator — paul-price.net

Paul Wolterink — The Netherlands
Designer/printmaker — paulwolterink.com

Penabranca — Brazil
Designer — penabranca.tumblr.com

Phickle — UK
Clothing label — phickleclothing.tumblr.com

Ping Pong Ping — Canada
Artists/design studio — pingpongping.ca

Post Projects — Canada
Art and design studio — post-projects.com

Poster Roast — UK
Retail — peopleofprint.com/collective/poster-roast/

Pouya Ahmadi — USA
Designer — pouyaahmadi.com

PPQ — UK
Fashion/clothing — ppqlondon.com

Print & Production London — UK
Print resource — print-and-production.info

Print Club London — UK
Printmakers/print studio — printclublondon.com

Print Liberation — USA
Printmaking and design studio — printliberation.com

Print Mafia — USA
Screenprint studio — printmafia.net

Printer of Dreams — UK
Printmaker — theprinterofdreams.com

Printorium — UK
Graphic designer — theprintorium.com

Printshop — USA
Screen printer — teamprintshop.com

Puck Studio — UK
Design collective — puckstudio.co.uk

R

Random House — Germany
Publisher — randomhouse.de

Reed Burgoyne — USA
Graphic designer/printmaker — reedburgoyne.com

Re:Surgo — Germany
Screenprint studio — resurgo-berlin.com

Ritty Tacsum — Malta
Photographer/multimedia artist — rittytacsum.com

Robert Bellamy Studio — Switzerland
Photographer — robertbellamy.com

Roderick Mills — UK
Illustrator/artist — roderickmills.blogspot.co.uk

Rollo Press — Switzerland
Print studio/publisher — rollo-press.com

Rose Thomas — UK
Printmaker — cargocollective.com/rosethomas

Ruta Daubure — UK
Illustrator — rutadaubure.com

Ryan Adair — USA
Designer/illustrator — theryanadair.com

Ryan Humphrey — UK
Artist — cargocollective.com/withapencilinhand

Ryan Len — Singapore
Visual communicator — behance.net/ryanlen

Ryan Todd — UK
Illustrator/designer — ryantodd.com

RYCA — UK
Artist — rcalla.otherpeoplespixels.com

S

Sabordage — France
Printmaker/publisher — sabordage.com

Sac Magique — Finland
Illustrator/graphic artist — sacmagique.net

Sagmeister & Walsh — USA
Design agency — sagmeisterwalsh.com

Salt — UK
Publisher/collective — saltsoapbox.com

Sam Hiscox — UK
Photographer/filmmaker — samhiscox.com

Sam Peet — UK
Illustrator/designer — sampeet.com

Samuel Esquire — UK
Illustrator/screen printer — samuelesquire.com

Sanna Annukka — UK
Illustrator/printmaker — sanna-annukka.com

Sarah Andreacchio — France
Illustrator — cargocollective.com/sarahandreacchio

Sarah Maycock — UK
Illustrator/artist — sarahmaycock.co.uk

Sarah Milton — UK
Printmaker — cargocollective.com/sarahmilton

Sarah Schrauwen — UK
Editor/book designer — sarahschrauwen.com

Sasa — Bosnia and Herzegovina
Illustrator/graphic designer — sasadesign.com

Saskia Pomery — UK
Artist/designer — saskiapomeroy.com

Savwo — UK
Print and design studio — savwo.co.uk

Sayle87 — UK
Designer/print experimenter — dansayle.com

Scott Campbell — USA
Designer — scttcmpbll.com/filter/work

Screen Stretch — UK
Screen-print supplier — screenstretch.co.uk

Serge Seidlitz — UK
Illustrator — sergeseidlitz.com

Serimal — Italy
Screen-printing studio — serimal.wordpress.com

Seripop — Canada
Screen printer/installator/sculpture — seripop.com

Shobo Shobo — UK
Fashion designer and retailer — shoboshobo.com

Signture Brew — UK
Beer/art/music — signaturebrew.co.uk

Simon Thompson — UK
Illustrator/printmaker — simon-john-thompson.com

Sleeperhold Publications — Belgium
Art publisher — sleeperholdpublications.com

Small Press — UK
Publisher — lesleysharpe.info

SNAP Studio — UK
Art and design collective — snapstudio.org.uk

Sneaky Raccoon — UK
Graphic artist/illustrator — sneakyraccoon.com

Snow Print — UK
Screen-printing studio — snowprint.co.uk

Soma Gallery — UK
Art and print gallery — somagallery.co.uk

Sonnenzimmer — USA
Printmaker/retailer — sonnenzimmer.com

Sophie Alda — UK
Illustrator — sophiealda.co.uk

SPANAKI — Greece
Designer/retailer — spanaki.gr

Spike Print Studio — UK
Print studio — spikeprintstudio.org

Squeegee & Ink — UK
Screen-printing studio — squeegeeandink.com

Steak MTN — USA
Designer — steakmtn.com

Stefanie Leinhos — Germany
Artist/illustrator — stefanie-leinhos.de

Steven Marsden — UK
Illustrator/mix-media artist — stevenmarsden.com

Stew Print Rooms — UK
Screen-print studio — stewprintrooms.blogspot.com

Struan Teague — UK
Artist/printmaker — struanteague.com

Studio 44 — UK
Online gallery/retailer — studiono44.tumblr.com

Studio Mothership — UK
Retailer — studiomothership.com

Sture Johannesson — Sweden
Graphic artist — sturejohannesson.com

Subform — The Netherlands
Graphic designer — subform.net

SuperBlast — Germany
Artist/graphic designer — superblast.de

Supermarket Sarah — UK
Retailer — supermarketsarah.com

Supermundane — UK
Multi-disciplinary designer — supermundane.com

Surfacephilia — UK
Surface design brand — surfacephilia.co.uk

Suzi Kemp — UK
Illustrator — suzikemp.com

T

T L — UK
Painter/printer — tl-tl-tl.com

Talia Levitt — USA
Painter — taliaelevitt.com

Tamara Elmallah — UK
Multi-disciplinary designer — tamara-elmallah.com

Tate Foley — USA
Printmaker/artist — tatemillerton.com

Team Print Shop — USA
Printer — teamprintshop.com

Telegramme — UK
Design studio — telegramme.co.uk

Telles — UK
Scarf label/retail — telles.co.uk

The Bear Cave — USA
Studio — bearcavestudio.tumblr.com/

The Daily Torygraph — UK
Publisher — dailytorygraph.com

The Design Ark — UK
Design blog — the-design-ark.com

The Grid System — USA
Graphic-design resource — thegridsystem.org

The Heads of State — USA
Graphic-design company — theheadsofstate.com

The Little Friends of Printmaking — USA
Printmaker — thelittlefriendsofprintmaking.com

The Positive Press — UK
Screen-print studio — thepositivepress.co.uk

The Predatory Bird Blog — UK
Design blog — thepredatorybird.com

The Print Project — UK
Letterpress studio — theprintproject.co.uk

The Print Shop — UK
Printer/retailer — thisisprintshop.co.uk

The Trip Control — UK
Illustrator/fashion label — angelinabeer.tumblr.com

The Typographic Cycle — UK
Organisation — typocircle.com

thekatielane — UK
Artist — thekatielane.com

theprintspace — UK
Photo-printing service — theprintspace.co.uk

They Magazine — UK
Contemporary art publication — theymagazine.com

Thomas Boswell — UK
Illustrator — cargocollective.com/thomasboswell

Thomas Whitcombe — UK
Designer — cargocollective.com/thomaswhitcombe

Till Hafenbrak — Germany
Illustrator — hafenbrak.com

Tim Gough — USA
Designer/art director — timgough.org

Tissue Magazine — Germany
Art publication — tissuemagazine.com

Tom Lacey — UK
Designer — tomlaceyart.tumblr.com

Tom Murphy — UK
Artist/printmaker — murphytom.com

Tom Radclyffe — UK
Illustrator — tradclyffe.co.uk

Tome Rowe — UK
Designer/illustrator — cargocollective.com/tomrowe

Topo Copy — Belgium
Open platform/publisher — topocopy.org

Transmission — UK
Visual communication studio — thisistransmission.com

Travis Stearns — USA
Designer — travisstearns.com

Tug Boat Print Shop — USA
Woodblock printer/retailer — tugboatprintshop.com

TurnbullGrey — UK
Letterpress and design studio — turnbullgrey.co.uk

Two Times Elliott — UK
Creative agency — 2xelliott.co.uk

Type Museum — UK
Typographic collection — typemuseum.org

Typeholics — Germany
Design studio — typeholics.de

Typoretum — UK
Letterpress studio — typoretum.co.uk

U

UK PosterAssociation — UK
Art organisation — ukposterart.com

Unruly Gallery — The Netherlands
Art gallery — unrulygallery.com

Urban Inks — USA
Screen printer/illustrator — urbaninks.com

V

Various & Gould — Germany
Artist/printmaker — variousandgould.com

Verity Keniger — UK
Printmaker — veritykeniger.co.uk

Vicki Johnson — UK
Printmaker — vickijohnsongetsprinting.blogspot.com

Victory Press — UK
Printer/publisher — victorypress.co.uk

Virassamy — Germany
Artist/illustrator — virassamy.org

Visual Editions — UK
Art publisher — visual-editions.com

W

Wallpapered — UK
Wallpaper printer — wallpapered.com

We Buy Your Kids — Australia
Exhibiting artists — wbyk.com.au

We Love Letterpress — UK
Letterpress studio — weloveletterpress.com

We Three Club — UK
Designer/screen printer — wethreeclub.com

WERKHAUS — UK
Art and design collective — werkhausltd.com

Whitney McVeigh — UK
Artist — whitneymcveigh.co.uk

Wonder Rollers — UK
Artist/photographer — wonder-rollers.tumblr.com

Word Collective — UK
Writers' collective — wordcollective.com

Wrap — UK
Art publication — thewrappaper.com

Y

YCN Shop — UK
Retailer — www.ycn.org

YES Gallery — USA
Gallery/shop/studio — yescincinnati.com

Yoshida & Co. — Japan
Cult brand — yoshidakaban.com

Young Monster — USA
Art collective/label — weareyoungmonster.com

Yoyo — UK
Illustrator/designer — weloveyoyo.com

Z

Zeena — UK
Textile designer — zeenashah.com

Zeloot — The Netherlands
Designer/illustrator — zeloot.nl

Zineswap — UK
Magazine and zine resource — zineswap.com

First published in the United Kingdom in 2015
by Thames & Hudson Ltd, 181A High Holborn,
London WC1V 7QX

Designed by Andy Cooke
Typeface: Aperçu by Colophon Foundry

British Library Cataloguing-in-Publication Data
A catalogue record for this book is available from
the British Library

ISBN 978-0-500-51781-9

Printed and bound in China by C&C Offset
Printing Co. Ltd

To find out about all our publications, please visit
www.thamesandhudson.com. There you can subscribe
to our e-newsletter, browse or download our current
catalogue, and buy any titles that are in print.